SOL WHITE'S HISTORY OF COLORED BASE BALL, WITH OTHER DOCUMENTS ON THE EARLY BLACK GAME 1886-1936

Compiled and Introduced by

JERRY MALLOY

University of Nebraska Press   *Lincoln & London*

SOL WHITE'S HISTORY OF COLORED BASE BALL, WITH OTHER DOCUMENTS ON THE EARLY BLACK GAME 1886-1936

© 1995 by the
University of Nebraska Press
All rights reserved
Manufactured in the
United States of America

⊖ The paper in this book meets
the minimum requirements of
American National Standard for
Information Sciences – Permanence
of Paper for Printed Materials,
ANSI Z39.48-1984.

Library of Congress Cataloging-in-Publication
Data appears on the last page of this book.

FRONTISPIECE.

Philadelphia Giants, 1905. Sol White's career reached its apogee with the Philadelphia Giants of 1905–7. This is one of the finest African American teams ever assembled. Pete Hill, an outfielder, was an outstanding player; Grant Johnson and Rube Foster wrote instructional essays on hitting and pitching for Sol White's *Guide*; Dan McClellan pitched black baseball's first perfect game. H. Walter Schlichter was the publisher of the *Guide*. *Back row*: Harry Smith; [unknown]; Harry Moore; Sol White, manager; Bill Francis; Dan McClellan. *Middle row*: Grant Johnson; Charlie Grant; H. Walter Schlichter; Rube Foster; Pete Hill. *Front row*: Bill Monroe, James Booker. Courtesy Negro Leagues Baseball Museum.

ENDPIECE.

Cuban Giants (also called Famous Cuban Giants, Original Cuban Giants, Genuine Cuban Giants, etc.) of 1905. *Back row*: [Ben?] Brown; [Bill?] Williams; J. M. Bright, manager; R. Best; Galloway. *Middle row*: Kelly; F. "Pop" Watkins; Gordon; Rawlins; Satterfield. *Front row*: Chase Lyons; Sampson; Bradley. Courtesy Negro Leagues Baseball Museum.

CONTENTS

ILLUSTRATIONS

ACKNOWLEDGMENTS

This project would be vastly inferior, indeed it might never have been published at all, were it not for the advice, guidance, information, and cooperation from a number of collaborators. The editor would like to express his appreciation to Dick Clark and his associates in the Negro Leagues Committee of the Society for American Baseball Research (SABR); the Dabney family; L. Robert "Bob" Davids of SABR; Craig Davidson and Refocus Films; Darci Harrington and Thomas R. Heitz of the National Baseball Hall of Fame in Cooperstown, N.Y.; Professor Lawrence D. Hogan; Larry Lester, Research Director, Negro Leagues Baseball Museum; and Robert W. Peterson, author of *Only the Ball Was White*, all of whom contributed to the assembly of this volume.

INTRODUCTION

SOL WHITE AND

THE ORIGINS OF

AFRICAN AMERICAN

BASEBALL

JERRY MALLOY

I returned, and saw under the sun, that the race is not to the swift, nor the battle to the strong, neither yet riches to men of understanding, nor yet favor to men of skill. But time and chance happeneth to them all. – Ecclesiastes 9:11–12

African American baseball is the national pastime's last historical frontier. In the past few decades, baseball history has been enriched by an impressive expansion of its base of researchers, writers, and avid students. The game itself is deeply ingrained in American society and tradition, having weathered the rigors of wars, depressions, and scandals and basked in the warm glow of more prosperous times. The intrinsic merit of its long, diverse history has been supplemented by the recent, widespread recognition of its value as an institutional lodestar, a point of reference throughout American life, relatively unchanged in its artistry and popular appeal since the Civil War era. As such, baseball has been embraced by the intellectual community and has attracted the scrutiny of professional historians who have made their way to the baseball diamond to help us understand the nation's economic, social, and racial past.

The history of African American baseball has benefited greatly from this emergent scholarship, as well as from the recent popular interest in the vibrant Negro Leagues of the 1920s through the 1940s. Negro League memorabilia and apparel have become commercially attractive. Organizations such as the Baseball Assistance Team and the Negro League Players Association have been formed to alleviate the financial burdens of several veterans of Negro League ball. An eagerly awaited Negro Leagues Baseball Museum is underway in Kansas City, Missouri, under the direction of John "Buck" O'Neil, longtime Negro League first baseman and manager who, as white baseball's first full-time black scout, lured Ernie Banks to the "Friendly Confines" of Chicago's Wrigley Field.

The Negro League Committee of the Society for American Baseball Research (SABR), under the leadership of Dick Clark, John B. Holway, and James A. Riley, has not only addressed but also nearly overcome the most daunting obstacle to public acknowledgment of Negro League excellence: the dearth of a statistical legacy. Negro League records have been painstakingly retrieved, box score by box score, game by game, year by year, from contemporary press accounts (both black and white), fulfilling the baseball public's appetite for numbers. Although there remains room for refinement, it is no longer correct to refer to the absence of a statistical record, with Negro League statistics readily available in such standard reference works as the *Baseball Encyclopedia* and *Total Baseball*. With such progress on the statistical legacy, SABR has encouraged the National Baseball Hall of Fame to grant Negro League stars the recognition they deserve by reforming the procedures that continue to discriminate against the men who have already suffered discrimination during their careers. A comprehensive encyclopedia of black baseball is near completion, and several notable figures in the history of African American baseball have been memorialized at their grave sites, thanks to the labors of SABR's Negro League Committee.

Since publication of Robert W. Peterson's groundbreaking *Only the Ball Was White* in 1970, important books addressing twentieth-century African American baseball have been written by historians such as Holway, Riley, Ocania Chalk, Donn Rogosin, Rob Ruck, Jules Tygiel, Janet Bruce, and James Bankes, and illustrations have been compiled by Robert D. Retort, Bruce Chadwick, and co-authors Phil Dixon and Patrick J. Hannigan. The result has been the rediscovery of an entire universe of black baseball, filled with more roles for African Americans than exist in baseball even today. For every Lou Gehrig, Walter Johnson, or Ty Cobb, there was a Buck Leonard, a Bullet Rogan, or an Oscar Charleston. But the world of black baseball also included African American managers, umpires, and sportswriters; African American executives, owners, and commissioners – and African American fans.

Baseball history's black component was long victimized by neglect. As early as 29 June 1895, an article in *Sporting Life* remarked that "nothing is ever said or written about drawing the color line in the [National] League. It appears to be generally understood that none but whites shall make up the League teams, and so it goes." But African American baseball history has all the merits of that of the mainstream white game, plus the complexity of operating within the din of racial animosity. It is a wonder that African American baseball was able to survive and a tribute to the creativity and diligence of those who enabled it to do so. The Negro Leagues became a source of pride within the African American community and have provided historians with a case study in black America's ability to create a vibrant subculture that fostered the standards and traditions of its mainstream counterpart, even in the face of racial scorn and hostility.

Despite the expansion of black baseball's historical universe, much remains to be done. Detailed accounts of specific players, teams, entrepreneurs, and events are required to complete our still-sketchy picture of the origins of black baseball. Since this is especially so in the case of nineteenth-century research, this new appearance of *Sol White's Official Guide: History of Colored Base Ball*, originally published in 1907, should increase historical awareness and provoke further research. This slender volume is still invaluable as a primary and a secondary source, a chronicle and a memoir, an elegy and an alarum, but its rarity has always been a problem for both the casual reader and the diligent scholar.

Those curious about African American baseball's early struggles to survive, much less thrive, in an increasingly harrowing racial environment are fortunate that White was present to record black professional baseball's first twenty years. He provides us with a unique window into the world of the men and events of black baseball's infancy. Sol White's *Guide* is the Dead Sea Scrolls of black professional baseball's pioneering community.

SOL WHITE, BALLPLAYER

No colored ball player has had a wider experience in base ball than Sol, and no ball player has profited by experience greater than he has. – H. Walter Schlichter (p. 8)

Sol White's considerable ability as a hard-hitting in-fielder during a period when ballplayers' careers (both black and white) tended to be peripatetic enabled him to move freely between the East and the Midwest to play for the best black baseball teams of his era. A review of his career as a ballplayer constitutes an overview of nineteenth-century black baseball.

THE MONEY PERIOD, 1885–1890

[1890] saw the close of a period in colored base ball which may well be called the money period. From 1885 until the close of 1890, colored base ball flourished.–Sol White (p. 20)

The figure of the African American in baseball has gone through various stages, from black players on white teams, to black teams in white leagues, to rivalry between independent black teams, to the formation of black leagues, to desegregation after World War II. The first African American player in baseball's sprawling minor leagues was John W. "Bud" Fowler, in Sol White's words, "the celebrated promoter of colored ball clubs, and the sage of base ball" (p. 74). Fowler, whose real name was John W. Jackson, was born in Fort Plain, New York, not far from Cooperstown, in 1858. Twenty years later he pitched three games in Lynn, Massachusetts, then proceeded to become one of the finest second basemen in the country in ten scattered minor-league seasons.

In 1884, when Fowler was on the Stillwater, Minnesota, North-western League team, Moses Fleetwood "Fleet" Walker, a bare-handed catcher, became the first African American in major-league baseball when his Toledo team joined the American Association, an

Integrated Keokuk team of 1885, with John "Bud" Fowler (center rear).
Courtesy National Baseball Library & Archive, Cooperstown, N.Y.

early rival of the National League. Fleet Walker's younger brother, Weldy, also played a handful of games for Toledo, although they never played together in any game. They would be the last African Americans in the major leagues until Jackie Robinson in 1947 and the last black brothers until Henry and Tommie Aaron in 1962.

The stream of black players entering the various white minor leagues widened in the mid-1880s (chapter 16). In 1885, Fowler and Fleet Walker played in three minor leagues, and the following year saw Fowler, Walker, George Stovey, Frank Grant, and Jack Frye in four such leagues. The zenith of this early experiment in interracial play, which was not altogether harmonious, occurred in 1887, "a banner year for colored talent in the white leagues," according

Moses Fleetwood "Fleet" Walker, Toledo catcher, 1883–84 seasons. Courtesy National Baseball Library & Archive, Cooperstown, N.Y.

to White (p. 76). Thirteen African Americans played that year on twelve white teams in five assorted eastern and midwestern minor leagues. Sol White and Weldy Walker were two of the four blacks in the Ohio State League that year, after having started the season as teammates on the Keystones, an early African American professional team from Pittsburgh.

But the most significant – and disquieting – events of 1887 occurred in the prestigious International League, just one level below

*Syracuse Stars, 1888. Champions of the International Association, the 1888
Stars had two of the league's three African American players (Fleet Walker
and Robert Higgins; Frank Grant played for Buffalo), down from seven the
previous year. Charlie Hackett had managed an all-black battery of George
Stovey and Fleet Walker in Newark N.J., in 1887, and signed Walker and
Higgins, a twenty-year-old, left-handed power pitcher and superb base runner,
when he took the helm at Syracuse the following season. Despite success on the
mound, Higgins left the team in 1889 and returned to Memphis, Tenn., where
he operated a successful barbershop for many years. Early researchers
occasionally misidentified Will Higgins as Syracuse's African American player.
Ed Dundon was one of several deaf nineteenth-century ballplayers.* Back row:
Moses Fleetwood Walker; Ed Dundon; McQuery; Frederick Ely; Will Higgins.
Middle row: *Oliver Beard; Cornelius Murphy; Wright; Charlie Hackett,
manager; Battin; Charles Marr.* Front row: *Robert Higgins, Albert Schellhase.
Courtesy Jim Rowe.*

the game's two major leages, the National League and the American
Association. Bud Fowler, Fleet Walker, George Stovey, Frank Grant,
Robert Higgins, William Renfro, and Randolph Jackson played at
one time or another for five International League teams that year.
Fowler and Renfro were teammates in Binghamton, New York,
while left-handed pitcher Stovey joined Walker in Newark, becom-

ing organized baseball's first African American battery. Stovey, who won thirty-four games that year (an International League record that still stands), and Grant, Buffalo's hard-hitting, slick-fielding second baseman, were among the best players in a league rich in talent. In a caption accompanying a portrait of Grant that appeared in Sol White's *Guide*, White declared that Grant was "the greatest base ball player of his age."[1]

Yet troubling racial episodes, fomented mostly by white players, occurred throughout the season. Most vexing were the symptoms of internal dissent on integrated teams, despite the obvious talent of the black players, ranging from intentional errors when a black teammate pitched to refusing to sit for team portraits including black players. *Sporting Life* (1 June 1887) asked, "How far will this mania for engaging colored players go? At the present rate of progress the International League may ere many moons change its name to 'Colored League.'" On 11 June, *Sporting News* noted that "a new trouble has just arisen in the affairs of certain of the baseball associations. It seems to have done more damage to the International [League] than to any other we know of. We refer to the importation of colored players into the ranks of that body." The *Toronto World* of 27 May 1887, under the headline "The Colored Ball Players Disgraceful," commented that a "number of colored players are now in the International League, and to put it mildly their presence is distasteful to the other players." White players, wrote the *World*, "dislike to play with these men," and this sentiment "may unexpectedly come to the front." They were right.

On 14 July, Cap Anson, major domo of Chicago's National League champions, demanded that Stovey be barred from pitching in an exhibition game at Newark. (Walker, Stovey's usual catcher, was not scheduled to play that day.) The same day, and probably not merely by coincidence, the directors of the International League announced that teams would not be allowed to sign African American players in the future. Sol White, as well as most writers after him, exaggerated Anson's role in the origin of the color line in nineteenth-century baseball. Robert Peterson was undoubtedly correct when he wrote, in *Only the Ball Was White*, "that [Anson] had the power and popularity to force Negroes out of organized baseball almost singlehandedly, as White suggests, is to credit him with more influence than he had, or for that matter, than he needed. For it seems clear that a majority of professional baseball players in 1887, both Northerners and Southerners, opposed integration in the game."[2]

Although the league allowed Walker to play through 1889, as well as Grant and Higgins in 1888, the writing was on the wall for African Americans in the International League, a wall that was descending across the sport, imposing an apartheid in baseball.

When Fleet Walker's younger brother Weldy read an erroneous report in *Sporting Life* that blacks would be banned from the Ohio State League's successor, the Tri-State League, he wrote an open letter to the league president denouncing the ruling as "a disgrace to the present age [which] casts derision at the laws of Ohio – the voice of the people – that says all men are equal." Black players, he argued, should be as welcomed by team owners with the same warmth accorded to the black patron's money (p. 81).

THE LIFER

[Sol White] has been close to the game since its beginnings in 1885 and he hardly talks about anything else. –Pittsburgh Courier, *12 March 1927 (chapter 10)*

Sol White, black baseball's first historian, was also one of its earliest "lifers." Although White played briefly for a few white teams, his playing career was predominantly within the world of African American baseball, which was gradually driven underground until it became invisible to the mainstream of white baseball. He was only nineteen years old when he was signed by the Pittsburgh Keystones in the tumultuous season of 1887, and for the next quarter century he traveled at the highest levels of African American baseball.

White was born in Bellaire, Ohio, directly across the Ohio River from Wheeling, West Virginia, and not far from Steubenville, Ohio, in the next county to the north, where Fleet and Weldy Walker grew up. As a youngster, White was a fan of the Globes, one of Bellaire's three white baseball teams, and the boyhood memory of his excitement at being pressed into emergency service from the sidelines for his first game with them was later embellished by the adult realization that the captain and second baseman of the Marietta, Ohio, team that the Globes were playing was none other than Byron Bancroft "Ban" Johnson, who would later found the American League (chapter 10).

In 1887, White entered the ranks of professional baseball with the Pittsburgh Keystones, charter members of the new, six-team League of Colored Base Ball Players (often called the National Colored Baseball League). The Cuban Giants, the country's first team of salaried black ballplayers, had attained "great prominence," wrote White, since their formation in 1885, which "led some people to think that colored base ball, patterned after the National League, with a team in every big league city, would draw the same number of people" (p. 12).

The new enterprise, a precursor to the Negro Leagues of the next century, was organized by Walter S. Brown, former Pittsburgh correspondent to the Cleveland *Gazette*, an African American weekly newspaper.[3] The League of Colored Base Ball Players was born in a series of meetings in Baltimore's Douglass Hall in the winter of 1886–87. At an early gathering, J. W. "Bud" Fowler, the pioneering black player, represented a group of potential investors from Cincinnati, where he worked as a barber in the off-season, but they never joined the league.[4] Also rejecting membership were the Cuban Giants, and the absence of this famous African American team from Trenton, New Jersey, was surely a deep disappointment to the circuit's backers.

To the surprise of many, the fledgling league was granted admission into baseball's official family when it was allowed to sign the National Agreement, the pact that defined the polity of so-called organized baseball. In reporting this, on 13 April, *Sporting Life* remarked on its pointlessness. The National Agreement, it explained, benefited signatories because "it guarantees a club undisturbed possession of its players. There is not likely to be much of a scramble for colored players [due to] the high standard of play required and to the popular prejudice against any considerable mixture of the races."

Nonetheless, the league opened its season at Recreation Park in

Cuban Giants, 1887. In June 1887 this team defeated major-league opponents in Cincinnati and Indianapolis. Back row: George Parago; Ben Holmes; Shep Trusty; Arthur Thomas; George Williams; Miller. Front row: William T. Whyte; Clarence Williams; Abe Harrison; S. K. Govern, manager; Ben Boyd; Jack Frye; Frank Allen. Courtesy National Baseball Library & Archive, Cooperstown, N.Y.

Pittsburgh on 6 May 1887. After "a grand street parade and a brass band concert," a crowd of 1,200 watched the Gorhams of New York City defeat the host Keystones, 11–8.[5] Less than two weeks later, the Keystones lost, 6–2, to the visiting Lord Baltimores in the final contest of the league's thirteen-game existence. Insufficient financing proved fatal. Boston's Resolutes folded while the team was in Louisville, stranding its players. "At last accounts," wrote the *Sport-*

ing News on 21 May, "most of the Colored Leaguers were working their way home doing little turns in barbershops and waiting on table in hotels."

A third of a century would pass before Rube Foster was able to forge a black league in 1920. Yet White points out that African American baseball benefited through this failed first attempt. "The short time of its existence served to bring out the fact that colored ball players of ability were numerous," he wrote. Furthermore, other than the Keystones and Gorhams, the league's teams were collections of local players in Boston, Philadelphia, Baltimore, and Louisville, who remained intact. "With reputations as clubs from the defunct Colored League, they proved to be very good drawing cards in different sections of the country" (p. 14). Several players, including Sol White, proceeded from the Colored League to play first for the higher-profile Gorhams and then the great Cuban Giants, among them Oscar Jackson, Andy Jackson, Robert Jackson (the latter two were brothers), William Malone, John Nelson, William Selden, Windsor Terrill, and John Vactor.

After the Colored League folded, White made his way back to Wheeling, West Virginia, where he played briefly with a local white club until being signed by the Wheeling team in white baseball's Ohio State League. He finished out the season playing fifty-two games at third base while hitting .370. In 1888 he returned to the Keystones, who played well in a four-team tournament in New York. Although the Cuban Giants won the contest, White recalled that "the surprise of the meet was the playing of the Keystones. Their only defeats were at the hands of the Cuban Giants; they won every game with the Gorhams and the Red Sox [of Norfolk, Va.]. The Keystones at this time were not professionals. They having one man other than home talent" (p. 16). That "one man," of course, was Sol White, and the larger fry of eastern black baseball quickly snatched from the Keystones the greatest player they ever had.

Not only was White on his way to eventually joining the mighty Cuban Giants, but for the next three seasons he played on African American teams in white baseball's minor leagues. During these years, the attention conferred on White in the local and national sporting press and the annual baseball guides of the era suggests

Cuban Giants of 1888. The center player in the front row may be Frank Grant, who played the last of his three consecutive seasons in Buffalo of the International League in 1888, suggesting that this photograph was taken in St. Augustine, Fla., the winter home of the Cuban Giants, before the start of the summer season. The Sporting News *wrote: "This club, with its strongest players on the field, would play a favorable game against such clubs as the New Yorks or Chicagos [of the white leagues]." Back row, left to right: Abe Harrison, George Stovey, Ben Holmes, Shep Trusty, Arthur Thomas, Ben Boyd. Middle row: William T. Whyte, George Williams, George Parago, Clarence Williams. Front row: Jack Frye, unknown (possibly Frank Grant), unknown. Courtesy John and Lillian Dabney.*

that he had considerable offensive ability. Standing 5 feet, 9 inches, and weighing 170 pounds, he eventually played all four infield positions, starting at third base and ending at first. White played five seasons in white baseball, never hitting lower than .324. In a composite of his 159 minor-league games, roughly equivalent to one long season, he hit a robust .356 in 683 at bats. His 243 hits included forty-two doubles, twelve triples, and seven home runs. He scored 174 runs and stole fifty-four bases (chapter 15). Ordinarily not so humble, White was surprisingly reticent in revealing his own considerable baseball talent, for clearly he was a player of major-league caliber.

He spent all of 1889 with the Gorhams of New York City. Owned by Ambrose Davis, the first African American owner of a salaried African American team, the Gorhams were perennial (and usually vanquished) early rivals of the Cuban Giants for black baseball supremacy in the East. In the year White played for the Gorhams, they represented Easton, Pennsylvania, in the Middle States League, which White mistakenly called the "Pennsylvania League." This association also included another African American team: the Cuban Giants of Trenton, New Jersey. White's team fared poorly and quit the league early, but the Cuban Giants challenged for the league title, and apparently won it, in what White called a "bitterly contested" pennant chase (p. 16). The "Cubes" (57–16) barely edged out Harrisburg (61–20) in winning percentage, .780 to .753. But a suspicious series of rulings on appealed games during the postseason winter meetings resulted in the adjustment of the totals to give Harrisburg a record of 64–19 (.771), just slightly ahead of the Cuban Giants's 55–17 (.764).[6]

THE COLORED MONARCHS OF YORK, 1890

The uniforms of the York "monarchs" are made of light Shaker gray flannel with black belt, trimmings and stockings. The word "York" will be across the breast of the shirts in black letters four inches deep. The caps will be neat and of new design, the side being pleated, which makes it stiff and it will always be in shape. A black button will ornament the top. Each player will be supplied with a leather bag in which to carry his suit. – York Gazette, 23 April 1890

Before the 1890 season, after four consecutive summers in Trenton, players from the Cuban Giants fled the penury of John M. Bright's ownership en masse to embrace the largess of J. Monroe Kreiter Jr. in York, Pennsylvania. The Cleveland *Gazette* (5 April 1890) lamented that "the famous Cuban Giants of '87, '88, and '89 will probably never again be seen in a team together." But Kreiter assembled most of these renegade Cuban Giants into a team he called the "Colored Monarchs of the Diamond" and gained for it

CLEVELAND GAZETTE, SATURDAY, AUGUST 23, 1890

W. T. WHYTE. P

J. Monroe Kreiter. Jr.
MANAGER.

W. JACKSON. C

A. HARRISON. SS

W. H. MALONE. P&F

G. L. WILLIAMS.
CAPT. & 3RD. B.

S. WHITE. 2ND B.

F. BOYD. C.F.

J. H. FRYE. 1ST B.

W. H. SELDEN. P&F.

A. THOMAS. C.

YORK INTER-STATE BASE BALL CLUB.
Formerly the Cuban Giants.

York Inter-State Base Ball Club, 1890 season. The Colored Monarchs of York, Pa., boasted Seldon, Malone, Thomas, Boyd, Whyte, Frye, Harrison, and Williams from John M. Bright's Cuban Giants. The team claimed a record of eighty-eight victories against twenty-seven defeats, playing in thirty-two towns in Pennsylvania and New Jersey before the Eastern Interstate League disbanded. Illustration from Cleveland Gazette *of 23 August 1890.*

admission into the Eastern Interstate League. (As he did with the Middle States League of the prior season, White mistakenly referred to this circuit as "the Pennsylvania League," p. 16.) While Bright stuffed his "Cuban Giants" uniforms with players of lesser talent, the *real* Cuban Giants were the team that White joined in 1890, the Monarchs of York.

Meanwhile, Harrisburg lured away Bright's slugging catcher,

Clarence Williams, then secured Frank Grant (who had played the previous three seasons in Buffalo) after a legal battle with York, occasioned by Frank's having signed with both teams. In July, Harrisburg jumped to the Atlantic Association, and the Eastern Interstate League expired within days. White praised Harrisburg's directors for their insistence that Grant be included in the team's interleague transfer, which was good for both Grant and the team (p. 18). But Clarence Williams was jettisoned to assuage the antipathy for black players expressed by the league's Baltimore, Jersey City, and Wilmington, Delaware, teams. "Williams has been released," reported the Cleveland *Gazette*, on 2 August 1890, "and the [Harrisburg] manager's only agreement was not to play or sign any other Afro-American player [besides Grant]."

THE BIG GORHAMS, 1891

This team, now known as the Big Gorhams, was without a doubt one of the strongest teams ever gotten together, white or black. Their ages ranging from 22 to 32; every man placed where he was strongest, pitchers and catchers strong in the field and at bat, every man a student of the game and experienced, they were a hard team for any club to beat. – Sol White (p. 20)

In 1891, Bright rounded up his prodigal Cuban Giants and entered them in the new Connecticut State League. There they represented Ansonia, Connecticut, until the league folded in June, ending forever the Cuban Giants's presence in organized baseball. Perhaps it was an ominous sign to be representing a city that was namesake to Cap Anson, early black baseball's bête noire. *Sporting Life* reported on 20 June that the league had been "in a disorganized condition almost from the start." The Cuban Giants's decidedly noncollegial behavior contributed mightily to this unhappy state. On 20 May, the team traveled to Princeton, New Jersey, for an exhibition game rather than play a scheduled league game in Meriden, Connecticut. This was the team's second no-show of the young season and a bitter disappointment to the many Meriden fans eager to salute Grant, who had starred there five years earlier, just before signing with Buffalo. On 30 May, the Waterbury *American* decried

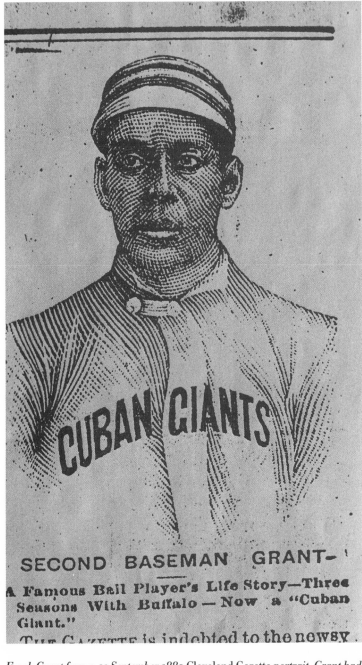

SECOND BASEMAN GRANT—

A Famous Ball Player's Life Story—Three
Seasons With Buffalo — Now a "Cuban
Giant."

THE GAZETTE is indebted to the newsy

Frank Grant from a 21 September 1889 Cleveland Gazette *portrait. Grant had
played ably for Buffalo of the International League from 1886 through 1889,
until discouraged by persistent racial hostility and contract disputes. Grant
went on to an impressive career with the Cuban Giants.*

the league's decision to include the supposed attraction of an African American team: "The Cuban Giants, representing Ansonia, as they conduct themselves at present, lend no strength to the league. They act as they see fit, paying not the slightest regard to schedule, the ordinary rules of the game or common decency. They were secured as a 'drawing card' and they have already begun to draw the wrong way. The Connecticut League has no use for them."

But by then, Bright's fealty to the struggling alliance had taken a back seat to more immediate concerns when, once again, his team began to lose ballplayers. After the Cuban Giants demolished Ambrose Davis's Gorhams, 18–10 and 17–2, in consecutive weeks in May, Davis responded with a tactic that would be repeated countless times in African American baseball's future: He simply gobbled up Bright's best players. But rather than wait for the end of the season, he embarked on the scheme immediately. George Stovey and Clarence Williams were the first to jump, joined later by White and Grant. On 13 June 1891, the Ansonia *Sentinel* wrote that "the Cuban Giants, or what remains of the original club, have gone to pieces and the Gorhams have absorbed the largest portion of the nine." Thus concluded the Cuban Giants's foray into organized baseball.

But J. M. Bright's misfortune was Ambrose Davis's finest hour. With the addition of Bright's Cuban Giants, Davis rechristened his revitalized team the Big Gorhams. Managed by former Cuban Giant skipper S. K. "Cos" Govern, the team's infield consisted of George Williams (first base), White (second base), Andy Jackson (third base), and Frank Grant (shortstop). Center fielder Oscar Jackson was flanked by one of the team's three pitchers, Stovey, William Selden, or William Malone, and one of its two catchers, Arthur Thomas or Clarence Williams. Every player on this team probably had skills equivalent to their major-league contemporaries.

White wrote that they lost only four games in more than a hundred, at one point winning thirty-nine straight – the Cleveland *Gazette* (29 August 1891) reported the string to be forty-one. Although *Sporting Life* (29 August 1891) wrote that their games "were mostly with weak amateur and semiprofessional teams," White ranked the

Big Gorhams the greatest black baseball team of the nineteenth century, comparing it with the powerhouse Philadelphia Giants of 1905, a team White later coowned, managed, and played for. "A series of games between these two teams," he mused, "would have been worth going miles to see and would have rivaled the [1906] world's series which was played in Chicago" (p. 89).

Despite the team's success on the field, the 1891 season was a failure at the gate. Bright failed to present a Cuban Giants team in 1892 for the first time since 1885. The outlook was so bleak for African American baseball that year that not one professional black team made it to the field. From this point on, White's career as a player receded somewhat into the historical mist, though its outlines remain visible. In the barren year of 1892, he rejoined the scaled-down Pittsburgh Keystones and also played for a team at the Hotel Champlain in Bluff Point, New York, formed by headwaiter Frank P. Thompson, one of the cofounders of the Cuban Giants in 1885 (chapter 10). In 1893 and 1894 he played for Bright's revived Cuban Giants, the only black professional team in the country in either season.

THE PAGE FENCE GIANTS, 1895

It took ten innings to decide the game yesterday afternoon between Bud Fowler's Page Fence Giants and the Findlays, and the winning run was made by Fowler himself. A large crowd was present, many being attracted by a desire to see Fowler and Grant Johnson, old-time Findlay players. – Findlay, Ohio, Daily Courier, 6 June 1895

White began the 1895 season with the Fort Wayne, Indiana, Western Interstate League team, but he later joined an African American team from the unlikely rural community of Adrian, Michigan, some fifty miles southwest of Detroit. This team, the Page Fence Giants, was one of the earliest black teams in the Midwest. The notion of an African American team in bucolic lower Michigan was the brainchild of the ubiquitous Bud Fowler, who cooked up the scheme the prior year while playing in Findlay, Ohio. He quickly won over twenty-year-old Findlay native Grant Johnson, Fowler's only black teammate. Tall, lean, and muscular, he came to be known as "Home Run" Johnson for his prodigious power. By the turn of the century he was African American baseball's preeminent shortstop and would remain so until the blossoming of John Henry Lloyd. Johnson's essay, "Art and Science of Hitting," appeared in White's *Guide* (pp. 100–102).

Fowler originally wanted to base his African American team in Findlay and call them the "Findlay Colored Western Giants," but he failed to secure the requisite backing. Instead, he went to Adrian and entered a partnership with two white businessmen, L. W. Hoch and Rolla I. Taylor. They formed a black baseball team that would advertise for two companies, including the Monarch Bicycle Company, a Massachusetts firm cashing in on the national cycling craze. (At the turn of the century, during the peak of that sport's American popularity, Marshall W. "Major" Taylor, an African American from Indianapolis, was cycling's fastest man on earth.)

Fowler's other benefactor was the Page Woven Wire Fence Company of Adrian. Page Fence was not unfamiliar with inventive promotional techniques. As a permanent demonstration of the capacity of its product to contain livestock, the company maintained a park in town stocked with various animals corralled by its woven-wire fencing. This menagerie was transported by rail to nearby county and state fairs with Page Fence cages, thus displaying the strength and versatility of the company's line of goods. Consequently, Page Fence fencing and cages were purchased by zoos around the world.

The Page Fence Giants had no home field, playing continuously on the road as a full-time barnstorming team based in Adrian. However, they traveled in a manner that Rube Foster would emulate when he created the glamorous Chicago American Giants in the second decade of the twentieth century. The Page Fence Giants's home on the road was an opulent, sixty-foot-long private rail coach. It was fitted with sleeping berths and a galley and serviced by a porter and a cook, thereby obviating difficulties inherent in obtaining lodging and meals during a time when public accommodations were subject to Jim Crow practices. Their coach pulled onto a sidetrack wherever the team was booked, the players preceded their games with a boisterous parade through town astride gleaming Monarch bicycles, dressed in black uniforms with "Page Fence

Findlay, Ohio, 1894 team. Grant Johnson was one of Findlay's few black residents. Back row: Harvey Pastorius; Fred Cook; Howard Brandenburg; Bill Reedy. Middle row: Grant Johnson; George Darby; Charles Strofel; Bobby Woods; Bud Fowler. Front row: F. Schwartz; Kid Odgen.

Giants" emblazoned in maroon letters — and topped off with firemen's caps provided by Monarch.

Augustus S. "Gus" Parsons, a hotel clerk and brother of one of Page Fence's directors, was the team's business manager, and he performed his duties well, booking the Page Fence Giants for 156 games in 112 towns of seven Midwest states. They won 118, lost 36, and tied 2, with 2 of their losses coming at the hands of the National League's Cincinnati Reds. Attendance varied from 800 to 7,100, for an average of 1,500 per game. In autumn the players traveled to Detroit for two games against an ad hoc team of players from five

Page Fence Giants railroad touring car. This photograph was taken 1 April 1895, shortly after the private coach arrived in Adrian, Mich., from the New Jersey builders. The sixty-foot-long, gilt-ornamented car was fitted with a lavatory, private manager's office, a state room, kitchen, and a combined dining-sitting-sleeping room. Capable of sleeping twenty, the car sported leather seats and a Belgian carpet. The coach was staffed with a cook (who pitched in one game) and a porter-barber. It not only advertised the team and its corporate sponsor but also helped the team avoid the problem of segregated public hotels and restaurants. Courtesy National Baseball Library & Archive, Cooperstown, N.Y.

National League teams. They won both games, 18–3 and 15–0, with George Wilson, who joined the team for this series, allowing just three hits while striking out fourteen in the latter. Some Detroit fans were persuaded that the Page Fence Giants were "the best team in Michigan."[7]

Bud Fowler's contacts enabled him to assemble what White called "a fine baseball team. They were hard to beat in '95 as their pitchers were among the best and their fielding excellent" (p. 24). The Giants signed some veterans of the Cuban Giants, such as White and Malone, and several exciting young players, like outfielder George Taylor and pitcher Joe Miller (both of whom were from Denver) and shortstop Grant Johnson. But Fowler's characteristic restlessness got the best of him, and he abandoned his creation on 15 July. He jumped to Adrian's entry in the Michigan State League for one game, then played thirty more with the Lansing team in the same league, hitting .331.

Adrian's white team, which won the league championship, was managed by Fowler's Page Fence partner Rolla Taylor and featured a black battery of Wilson and Vasco Graham. Wilson, a nineteen-year-old native of Palmyra, Michigan, pitched for the Page Fence Giants the following year and went on to a career in African American baseball, mostly in the West, so distinguished as to earn White's encomium as the black game's equivalent of the great Rube Waddell (p. 65). For three weeks in 1895, Wilson and Graham were even teammates of Honus Wagner.

White left the team after one year. But Grant Johnson and George Taylor remained and the Page Fence Giants signed several talented players, such as outfielder George Wilson and Charlie Grant. The latter, unrelated to Frank Grant, was White's replacement at second base. In 1896 they soundly defeated a Cuban X-Giants team that included White in a series of fifteen games played in several towns in southern Michigan, winning ten of them (p. 37). The Page Fence Giants prospered on the field but began to struggle at the gate. Since they were always traveling, press coverage in Adrian became sparse. They dissolved after the 1898 season, only to be reborn in 1899 as the Chicago Columbia Giants.

THE CUBAN X-GIANTS, 1896

We are informed legally that the name of Cuban X-Giants is not incorporated and that we have a perfect right to the use of same. – E. B. Lamar,
Sporting Life, *11 April 1896*

In 1890 White had joined the stampede to York, Pennsylvania, which eviscerated the proud Cuban Giants of J. M. Bright. He did so again the following year, leading the exodus to the Big Gorhams. Now, in 1896, White was a key player in the final abandonment of Bright's parsimony when he and his teammates finally found an owner more to their liking, Edward B. "E.B." Lamar Jr. of Brooklyn. In summarizing Bright's role in nineteenth-century African American baseball, White called him "a lover of the game and a money-getting baseball man, . . . the leading spirit of his day in keeping the game before the public."

> "J.M.," as he was called by his players, was extremely selfish in his financial dealings and naturally shrewd. . . . [H]is players were always called upon to help him in an idea. When it came to getting money, "J.M." was full of ideas. He held up many games after his team reached a ground with a packed stand and demanded a boost in his stipulated guarantee. He generally got what he asked for. Bright spent his life in colored baseball, and he was not a millionaire when he died. (chapter 11)

Unlike Bright, E. B. Lamar "spent his time and mind in making the game a lucrative calling for ball players."[8] The result was one of American sport's most curiously named teams, not to mention a new eastern powerhouse in African American baseball. Lamar, whose brother Pete caught two games with the Chicago Cubs in 1902 and one with the Boston Red Stockings five years later, christened his team of ex–Cuban Giants the "Cuban X-Giants," creating no small confusion for both contemporary fans and future historians. For the next decade, the Cuban X-Giants would be among the best black teams in the East, while Bright's team carried on under the name of "Genuine" or "Original Cuban Giants." During the late 1890s, the two teams hurled various boastful claims and defiant challenges at each other during a rivalry in which the Cuban Giants were usually slightly inferior to their rival, much as the Gorhams had been to the Cuban Giants of the prior decade.

White closed out the century with the Cuban X-Giants. Following the 1899 season, the Xs played a series against the Chicago Columbia Giants. "Fourteen games were played in and around Chicago, the crowds on several occassions being enormous," White wrote. "The games were hotly contested all through the series but the superior hitting of the Cuban X-Giants won for them the title of Champions. They won nine of fourteen games played" (p. 38). The Columbia Giants were born that season of the remnants of the Page

Fence Giants and managed by former Page Fence player John Patterson. To avenge the Columbia Giants's defeat, Patterson signed White for 1900.

THE CHICAGO COLUMBIA GIANTS, 1900

The Columbia Giants [of 1900] were stronger in the box than the Unions and made less errors in their fielding. These qualifications won for the Columbia Giants, the local Championship of Chicago and a big bunch of money. Of the five games played, the "Unions" did not win a game. – Sol White (p. 38)

In a sense, this team was a throwback to African American baseball's earliest era in that it represented a black middle-class group in Chicago, the Columbia Social Club. For early black teams such as the Pythians and Excelsiors of Philadelphia, the Uniques and Monitors of Brooklyn, and the Mutuals of Washington DC, ballgames against similar clubs were little more than festive social romps, a sufficient excuse for the smashing buffet that inevitably followed. But by 1899, a new breed of upscale black professionals preferred simply to buy good players to nurture the honor and good name of the Columbia Social Club.

The Columbia Giants played at Wentworth Avenue and Thirty-ninth Street (now the intersection of the Dan Ryan Expressway and Pershing Road), just a few blocks south of the current incarnation of Comiskey Park, in the former grounds of the Chicago Cricket Club and future home of both Charles Comiskey's Chicago White Sox and Rube Foster's Chicago American Giants. Their players luxuriated in the extravagance of two sets of uniforms, whites for home games and grays for the road. Columbia Social Club members dispensed a generous amount of disposable income in outfitting its sporting representatives. Altogether, wrote White, "they were the finest and best equipped colored team that was ever in the business" (p. 28).

Chicago was the nation's powerhouse city in black baseball the year White played for the Columbia Giants. "While the Unions [another black team from Chicago] were thrashing the Cuban X-Giants, of New York, the Columbia Giants were walloping the Genuine Cuban Giants, of New York" (p. 38). In 1901, White returned East permanently, signing with the Cuban X-Giants.

White continued his career as a player until 1909, when he was forty-one years old. Indeed, in 1905 he teamed with Charlie Grant (second base), Grant Johnson (shortstop), and Bill Monroe (third base) in one of the finest infields of all time. This was the Philadelphia Giants club that White rated as the best team since the Big Gorhams of 1891. One need not cast aspersions on White's impartiality in rating two teams he played for so highly. He was, after all, a very good player. But his devotion to the Philadelphia Giants was accompanied by a special pride, for this brilliant team was assembled by White himself in his new role in African American baseball, that of team owner.

THE PHILADELPHIA GIANTS, 1902–1909

[A] careful investigation of the playing record of the Philadelphia Giants will show that they have earned the right to play against the best white teams for they can put up an article of base ball that is as good as the best and at any stage of the game they could make either the [Philadelphia] Athletics or the New York [Giants], hustle to win out. Of course, there is a possibility of the colored men winning and that would be distasteful to many followers of the white team, but true sport recognizes no color nor clan and it should always be, may the best man win. – Sol White (p. 51)

In 1902 Sol White entered a partnership with two white sportswriters from Philadelphia, H. Walter Schlichter and Harry Smith, to form the Philadelphia Giants. Schlichter, who later published *Sol White's Official Guide*, was the team's business agent, while White tended to matters on the field. For eight years, they operated one of the dominant eastern black teams in the bustling African American baseball industry.

The days were gone when one eastern team could dominate black baseball, as the Cuban Giants and the Cuban X-Giants had done so often from the late 1880s through the 1890s. Gone, too, were the dismal times of 1892 to 1894, when there was, at most, just one black professional team in the country. As the new century dawned, African American baseball blossomed with a profusion of new teams. By the time White wrote his *Guide* following the 1906 season, he could list nine such professional teams (plus two Cuban teams) within a hundred miles of that Queen Mother of African American baseball cities, Philadelphia (p. 31). It is doubtful that many of these teams made much (if any) money, but the proliferation of teams suggests at least a thriving market for black baseball.

Both before and after, some African American teams were owned for reasons other than profits. The Page Fence Giants, as we have seen, were little more than a corporate advertising campaign, and the Chicago Columbia Giants existed primarily to adorn the prestige of a black social club. Similarly, John W. Connor formed the Brooklyn Royal Giants in 1906 to promote his Royal Cafe and Palm Garden, an advertiser in *Sol White's Official Guide*.[9] In the future, Gus Greenlee would create the celebrated Pittsburgh Crawfords in the early 1930s as an embellishment of his Crawford Grill. Connor and Greenlee acquired African American teams to concoct a glamorous blend of sports, entertainment, and society – as if, say, a Toots Shor had aspired to own the New York Yankees in the 1950s.

MANAGERS' TROUBLES

The tribulations of a manager of the base ball team, especially in a colored team, are known only to those who have inside knowledge of the game and are familiar with what a base ball manager has to contend.
– Sol White (p. 67)

In the first twenty years of the twentieth century, African American baseball was conducted within a context of frequent – indeed, bewildering – player movement among teams. As John Henry Lloyd, the "black Honus Wagner," later said, "Where the money was, that's where I was," and he certainly was not alone in this mercenary sentiment. Black baseball never developed anything similar to the white game's now-discredited reserve clause, which bound each player to a single team. African American ballplayers, unencumbered by such occupational slavery, became what we would now call unrestricted free agents after every season.

A few teams, even in the nineteenth century, were able to staff developmental teams. The Big Gorhams, for example, employed such a team, called – not surprisingly – the Little Gorhams (p. 20). But black baseball never had a minor-league system. New players, often recruited while on tour in games against black or integrated amateur, semipro, town, college, or industrial league teams, had to be ready to jump directly into the highest level of performance to enter the ranks of big-time African American baseball. Star players, in the absence of a reserve clause, were ready, willing, and able to exploit a seller's market, a circumstance bemoaned by White in a section he called "Managers Troubles."

> In this day and time, when colored base ball teams are numerous and each striving for supremacy, the colored manager's path is not one of sunshine. With twelve or fourteen men under his command, twelve or fourteen different minds and dispositions to control and centre on the intricate points of play, with no National League of base ball clubs behind the rules and regulations, with the many complaints of players and threats of quitting ringing in his ears day after day, he passes many a sleepless night and will often ask for that "Patience he needs." (pp. 67–68)

At the core of the first Philadelphia Giants team were shortstop Frank Grant, catcher Clarence Williams, third baseman Bill Monroe, and outfielder Andrew "Jap" Payne. The following year, 1903, they were defeated for the "colored championship" by a strong Cuban X-Giants team that included shortstop Grant Johnson, catcher Chappie Johnson, pitcher Danny McClellan, and rookie Preston "Pete" Hill, one of the finest outfielders in the pre–Negro Leagues era, a player with great speed and occasional power. But the dominating factor in the series was the pitching of a strapping young southpaw from Calvert, Texas, named Andrew "Rube" Foster. Foster threw a three-hitter in a 3–1 victory in the opener, the first of his four victories in the series, as the X-Giants beat White's team five games to two (p. 40).

Following the established principle of "if you can't beat 'em, buy 'em," White reacted by hiring Foster, McClellan, Hill, and Chappie Johnson from the Cuban X-Giants in 1904 and replacing Frank Grant with Charlie "Tokohama" Grant, so nicknamed because John McGraw, while managing Baltimore's American League team in

1901, unsuccessfully conspired to foist him on white baseball as a Cherokee by that name (pp. 78–79). The 1904 Philadelphia Giants won all four games against the International League's Newark Bears, then run by Ed Barrow, future owner of the New York Yankees. They won the black baseball championship in Atlantic City, winning two of three games from the Cuban X-Giants, in a series in which "both players and spectators were worked to the highest pitch of excitement. Never in the annals of colored baseball," wrote White, "did two nines fight for supremacy as these teams fought" (p. 44). Once again, Foster was the key to victory. He struck out eighteen and allowed but three hits in the opener, then shut them down on just two hits in game three. He also led the Phils in hitting, with a .400 batting average.

What made the 1905 team the greatest of White's Philadelphia Giants was the addition of Home Run Johnson, the Cuban X-Giants's last remaining star. But Johnson left the Philadelphia Giants after just one year to manage Connor's new Brooklyn Royal Giants. Also in 1906, White lost catcher Chappie Johnson to the crosstown-rival Quaker Giants. White signed Nat Harris and Bill Francis for his infield and the Philadelphia Giants won 134 games while losing only 21. They clinched a four-way battle for supremacy in the East on Labor Day before a crowd of 10,000 fans in the Philadelphia Athletics's Columbia Park, "the largest crowd of spectators that ever attended a base ball game between colored teams," wrote White (p. 33). This also was the first game between African American teams in a major-league ballpark. Flush with victory, Schlichter offered to take on the winners of the white "world's series" to "decide who can play base ball the best – the white or the black American," but the challenge went unanswered (p. 49).

The beginning of the end came in 1907, when Foster jumped to the Leland Giants of Chicago and took Pete Hill and three other players with him. White responded by signing catcher Bruce Petway from the Brooklyn Royal Giants and, more important, John Henry Lloyd, the game's greatest shortstop. The following year, White took the Philadelphia Giants west to play the Chicago Leland Giants. White beat Foster's team four straight games in Detroit, and Foster refused to play the final three scheduled games in Chicago.

The vengeful Foster did not allow White much time to gloat. In 1909, he signed both Lloyd and Petway from Philadelphia. Although White was able to discover yet another fine player, speedy Spotswood Poles (called "the black Ty Cobb"), after 1908 it was all over for the Philadelphia Giants.

In 1907, White had called Foster "one of the best colored pitchers the game has produced," so good, in fact, that he asked Rube to write a section in his *Guide* on "How to Pitch" (pp. 96–100). But Foster would go on to play a much bigger role than that of a dominating lefthanded pitcher. The paterfamilias of the Negro Leagues, Foster had a career that would rival in variety and magnitude the achievement of white baseball's Al Spalding and Charles Comiskey combined, even serving as commissioner, unlike Spalding and Comiskey.

Just as White had destroyed the Cuban X-Giants by stealing John Henry Lloyd in 1905, so too Foster lured Lloyd from White in 1909, with a similar result. White's Philadelphia team was just one of the early victims of Rube Foster's ambition. Within a few years, he would nudge Frank Leland out of the picture in Chicago and found the Chicago American Giants, the most magisterial African American sporting organization of its time and a creation so closely identified with its creator that it was often called simply "Foster's Giants." In 1920 Foster founded the Negro National League, an alliance White could merely contemplate in 1907. Foster even fought white booking agent Nat Strong to a standstill, with Strong agreeing to undisturbed control of eastern black baseball in exchange for giving Foster a free hand in the Midwest. It was only Foster's mastery at booking that prevented Strong from controlling all of big-time African American baseball.

The year 1911 found White in Harlem, managing the Lincoln Giants, owned by white boxing promoter Jess McMahon and his brother Rod. White brought Spotswood Poles with him and signed several star players, including pitchers Smokey Joe Williams and Dick "Cannonball" Redding, catcher Luis Santop, and infielders John Henry Lloyd and Grant Johnson. But this team dissolved in July and Sol White headed back home to Bellaire, Ohio. There

John Henry Lloyd in Brooklyn Royal Giants uniform.
Courtesy Robert W. Peterson.

Frank Leland. Courtesy National Baseball Library & Archive,
Cooperstown, N.Y.

he lived removed from the world of baseball for eight long years,
working in some unknown capacity.

When Rube Foster founded the Negro National League (NNL) in
1920, White served as secretary of the Columbus, Ohio, team. In
1924 he managed the Cleveland Browns of the NNL (alas, to a last-
place finish), and two years later he coached the Newark Stars of
the Eastern Colored League, the eastern component in the 1920s of

1909 Leland Giants, Rube Foster is on the far right, back row.
Courtesy National Baseball Library & Archive, Cooperstown, N.Y.

Composite photograph with the 1915–16 Royal Poinciana team (top) and 1914
Breakers Hotel team (bottom). Smoky Joe Williams is third from right, bottom
row. Courtesy National Baseball Library & Archive, Cooperstown, N.Y.

what we now call the Negro Leagues. But Sol White's impact on the game on the field was greatly diminished. He retained his enthusiasm for African American baseball and provided several helpful and informative newspaper articles for two black newspapers in New York, the *Age* and the *Amsterdam News*, which are transcribed in chapters 10, 11, and 12.

He lived in Harlem for the final third of his life, where he continued to follow the course of African American baseball and extol its history. In the 1930s he worked to secure Yankee Stadium as the home field for an African American team. He told the *Pittsburgh Courier* that he "like[d] to go to the library and read good books" (Chapter 10). He lived long enough to see the first African American major leaguer in sixty-three years when Jackie Robinson joined the Brooklyn Dodgers in 1947. It is believed White died in New York City in 1955, at age eighty-seven, though his death record remains undiscovered and his place of burial unknown. Nor is it known if he ever married or had any children.

SOL WHITE, HISTORIAN

I have endeavored to follow the mutations of colored base ball, as accurately as possible, from the organization of the first colored professional team in 1885, to the present time, in the trust that it will meet the approbation of all who may peruse the contents of this book.— Sol White (p. 3)

Nothing is known about White's childhood education in Bellaire. But, as the (black) Chicago *Broad Ax* wrote on 7 August 1909, he later had "the reputation of being the only professional Negro player who is a college graduate, having been educated at Wilberforce university, which is the oldest institution in America for the education of Afro-Americans." Wilberforce, named after England's foremost abolitionist, was founded in Xenia, Ohio, in 1856 by the African Methodist Episcopal Church.

Although it is doubtful that White graduated with a college degree, Wilberforce's records indicate that in the 1896–97 academic year he was a third-year student in the English preparatory department, though he may have begun his studies just the year before at the second-year level. He was also a private in the Corps of Cadets, the commandant of which was Lieutenant Charles Young, only the third African American to graduate from West Point. Young, who was in Wilberforce as an instructor of military science, eventually rose to the rank of lieutenant colonel after leading the all-black Tenth U.S. Cavalry Regiment with distinction during General John Pershing's pursuit of Pancho Villa into Mexico in 1916. Yet he faced discrimination in the military just as surely as White did in baseball. When the United States entered World War I, Army doctors declared Young unfit for active duty because of high blood pressure, which Young refuted by riding 500 miles on horseback from Wilberforce to Washington DC in sixteen days. Still, the Army held its ground and did not activate him until five days before the war ended.

One can only imagine how the gregarious White must have enthralled his fellow scholars with yarns from his summers spent playing baseball for the Page Fence Giants and the Cuban X-Giants. He received high grades in a curriculum that included reading, grammar, arithmetic, physiology, history, elocution, spelling, and U.S. history. Meanwhile, he developed the innate interest in history that ultimately made him the Livy of African American baseball.

The original edition of *Sol White's Official Base Ball Guide* was physically quite small, its 128 pages measuring only 5¾ by 3½ inches. Included were fifty-seven priceless photographs of various teams, players and executives, and even one of entertainer Bert Williams, who teamed with George Walker in one of the most popular song-and-dance comedy teams of the era. The (quite informal) Williams and Walker Base Ball Club antedated Bill "Bojangles" Robinson's later investment in the more formidable New York Black Yankees in the 1940s.[10]

The book was underwritten with fourteen pages of advertisements, with three on each of two pages, two on each of two other pages, and ten full-page ads. Almost all of the advertising was purchased by Philadelphia business concerns, though Connor, owner of the Royal Giants, bought a page proclaiming his flagship enterprise, the Royal Cafe and Palm Garden of Brooklyn. Purveyors of alcohol and tobacco, who embraced the trade of the sporting set, predominate the roster of twenty advertisers, but the availability of Kimball's Anti-Rheumatic Ring, for those requiring "a general warming, quickening, strengthening and equalization of the circulation," was also announced. Two Philadelphia daily newspapers also advertised: the (white) *Item*, whose sports editor was Schlichter, and the (black) *Tribune*, half of whose page of space is allotted to a portrait of its city editor, G. Grant Williams.

The book was edited and published by Schlichter, White's Philadelphia Giants partner. In a caption accompanying a photograph of Schlichter, White identified him as the president of the "National Association of Colored Baseball Clubs of the United States and Cuba."[11] This vaguely structured association, one of a handful of failed efforts to create a black baseball league prior to Rube Foster's success in 1920, lasted only one year. "Slick," as Schlichter was called, was lauded by White for "his ability as a press agent and booster" (p. 49). Sol White's *Guide* may have been produced, at least in part, as a promotional booklet for the Philadelphia Giants, then at the apogee of their existence. Schlichter also was in business with the influential New York booking agent Nat C. Strong, as revealed in an advertisement.[12] Strong himself is identified in a photograph as the secretary of the aforementioned "National Association."[13] In a 1936 letter to Sol White, Schlichter said that Strong was the only man he knew who made money on African American baseball. "And at that, I am better off than he is now," he remarked, sounding very much like an embittered former partner. "I am still living and have my health and Nat didn't take his wealth with him. There is no pocket in a shroud, you know" (chapter 13).

Schlichter published *Sol White's Official Base Ball Guide* when White was at the apex of what the *Pittsburgh Courier* later called "the heyday of his glory of 1905, 06, and 07" (chapter 10). Within the context of African American baseball, this was certainly true. But it was hardly a glorious time for all but a few of the country's black citizens. Rayford W. Logan's *Negro in American Life and Thought* (1954) was ominously subtitled *The Nadir, 1877–1901*; a revised edition in 1965 was retitled *The Betrayal of the Negro: From Rutherford B. Hayes to Woodrow Wilson.* With Jim Crow ascendant, the history of African Americans of this sad era is a chronicle of despair.

A BARE-HANDED CATCHER'S HOME COLONY

The Negro never can be raised to an equal point in civilization while occupying his isolated position in the United States. – Moses Fleetwood Walker, 1908 [14]

The year after White's *Guide* appeared, Moses Fleetwood Walker, the bare-handed catcher who had entered the white man's preserve of major-league baseball in 1884, wrote a book having nothing to do with baseball. *Our Home Colony: A Treatise on The Past, Present and Future of the Negro Race in America*, published in Steubenville, Ohio, was a radical separatist tract that prescribed black emigration and a precursor to black-nationalist leader Marcus Garvey's "back-to-Africa" campaign. Walker's outlook was far more despondent than White's. The alarmingly commonplace practice of lynching illustrated to Walker that American racism "has reached such a degree of virulence that under its influence reasoning men perform like wild animals [with] the most horrible example of barbarism in a civilized country the world has ever seen." The so-called Negro problem, he averred, would more aptly be referred to as "the white man's Problem, for its solution . . . rests almost entirely with him."[15]

Walker, who attended Oberlin College for three years and the University of Michigan for one, concluded that "the Negro race will be a menace and the source of discontent as long as it remains in large numbers in the United States. The time is growing very near," he warned, "when the whites of the United States must either settle this problem by deportation, or else be willing to accept a reign of terror such as the world has never seen in a civilized country." Since African Americans are "alien and always will be regarded as such in this country," the "only practical and permanent solution of the present and future race troubles in the United States is entire separation by Emigration of the Negro from America. Even forced

Emigration would be better for all than the continued present relations of the races."[16]

While Walker's views were extreme, there was no question that African Americans had been relentlessly and systematically deprived of opportunity and hope throughout American life and thought, despite the nation's self-designation as a paragon of equality and justice in the community of nations. In housing, education, and employment, in politics, government, and law, in literature, science, and philosophy, indeed, everywhere one turned, thoroughgoing racist policies and practices had stripped the African American of justice and dignity, from matters trivial to vital, and proclaimed the United States to be "a white man's country."

As if the terrorist campaigns of the Ku Klux Klan did not sufficiently demonstrate the triumph of white supremacist rule in the South, where 90 percent of the country's black population still resided, politicians pandered to Negrophobia to garner lily-white voters, once black disfranchisement was complete in the former Confederate states. James K. Vardaman, campaigning for governor of Georgia in 1900, defended lynching as an antedote to rape, saying, "We would be justified in slaughtering every Ethiop on the earth to preserve unsullied the honor of one Caucasian home." Vardaman denounced the African American as a "lazy, lying, lustful animal which no conceivable amount of training can transform into a tolerable citizen."[17]

In 1905, Georgia's Tom Watson voiced the callous attitude of many whites when he wrote, "What does Civilization owe to the negro? Nothing! Nothing!! Nothing!!!"[18] When Benjamin R. "Pitchfork Ben" Tillman, the "one-eyed plowboy," was elected governor of South Carolina in 1890, he proclaimed that "the triumph of . . . white supremacy over mongrelism and anarchy is most complete."[19] Later, as a U.S. senator, he ridiculed northerners for their hypocrisy (and probably made many squirm with guilt) after a three-day rampage of frenzied mob violence in Springfield, Illinois, home to Abraham Lincoln, in 1908 (a catalyst in the creation of the National Association for the Advancement of Colored People). So much for "the brotherhood of man," sneered the supercilious Tillman:

1 : *Jerry Malloy*

The brotherhood of man exists no longer because you shoot negroes [*sic*] in Illinois, when they come in competition with your labor, as we shoot them in South Carolina when they come in competition with us in the matter of elections. You do not love them any better than we do. You used to pretend that you did, but you no longer pretend it, except to get their votes.[20]

Pseudoscientific theories misapplied Charles Darwin's principles of evolution, investing assertions of Caucasian superiority with a false patina of intellectual respectability. Thus, Charles Carroll wrote *The Negro A Beast* in 1900, and Robert W. Shufeldt's *The Negro, A Menace to American Civilization* was published in 1907, the same year that Sol White's *Guide* appeared. In 1906, Thomas Ryan Dixon wrote *The Clansman*, a best-selling novel set in South Carolina during Reconstruction that portrayed the African American in the most bestial terms. Nine years later, filmmaker D. W. Griffith used the novel as the basis of the first feature-length American movie, *The Birth of a Nation*, which was received with popularity and acclaim. Although it achieved technical and artistic virtuosity, the film's distortions and outright lies misinformed entire generations about the role of African Americans in the Reconstruction South. Woodrow Wilson, a friend of Dixon's from their college years, arranged for a private screening of the film at the White House and said it "wrote history with lightning."[21] In truth, though, art was merely the handmaiden of outrageous calumny.

THE STRANGE CAREER OF SOL WHITE

[Sol White's] object in telling his story is to let some of the younger fellows know something of what is behind them – something of the struggles that have made possible the improved conditions of the present.
– Pittsburgh Courier, 12 March 1927 (chapter 10)

Yet race relations in the country had not always been so repressive, as the history of nineteenth-century baseball indicates. Sol White was a member of a tragic generation of African Americans, born within a few years of the Civil War. He and his contemporaries reached adulthood at a time, in the mid-1880s, when the brutal protocols of racial discrimination that soon would follow seemed by no means inevitable. It was, as C. Vann Woodward remarked in *The Strange Career of Jim Crow*, "a twilight zone that lies between living memory and written history," when "old and new rubbed shoulders – and so did black and white – in a manner that differed significantly from Jim Crow of the future or slavery of the past."[22] "It was a time of experiment, testing, and uncertainty – quite different from the time of repression and rigid uniformity that was come toward the end of the century. Alternatives were still open and real choices had to be made."[23]

Sol White illustrated this development in baseball in a section titled "The Color Line." "In no other profession," he wrote, "has the color line been drawn more rigidly than in baseball" (p. 74). Yet White was able to recall a time, twenty years earlier, when the rules of racial engagement had been far less severe. The realm of public accommodations provides a clear example. The black player, he noted, "suffers great inconvenience, at times, while travelling," caused by the refusal of innkeepers to lodge African Americans. "The situation is far different today in this respect than it was years ago. At one time the colored teams were accommodated in some of the best hotels in the country, as the entertainment in [1887] of the Cuban Giants at the McClure House in Wheeling, W. Va., will show." Furthermore, "such proceedings on the part of hotel-keepers . . . will be difficult to remedy" (p. 78) – difficult, indeed.

In 1875 Congress legislated that "all persons within the jurisdiction of the United States shall be entitled to the full and equal enjoyment of the accommodations . . . of inns, public conveyances on land or water, theaters and other places of public amusement; subject only to the conditions and limitations established by law and applicable alike to citizens of every race or color." But in 1883, the U.S. Supreme Court ruled that such legislation was not sanctioned by the citizenship provisions of the Fourteenth Amendment to the Constitution. (When Congress passed the Civil Rights Act in 1964, virtually identical in purpose to the 1875 legislation, it avoided putting the Supreme Court in the inelegant position of reversing itself by basing it on the Constitution's interstate commerce clause rather than on the Fourteenth Amendment.)

As a result, people in such positions as railroad conductors, ticket sellers, and hotel desk clerks gradually came to establish and enforce each community's racial boundaries. Through the Supreme Court's judicial sophistry, a law clearly intended to protect minority groups from racial discrimination was contorted into a ruling that threw open the door to Jim Crow codes. The Court's interpretations of the Fourteenth Amendment during the Gilded Age gratuitously shifted its benefits from black citizens to private corporations, thus abandoning African Americans to the tender mercies of implacable foes. In doing so, the Court may have helped white Americans heal the deep sectional wounds inflicted by the Civil War and Reconstruction, but white harmony was purchased, at a very steep price, with the coin of black repression.

The crippling effect of the ruling in the civil rights cases on the care and feeding of African American baseball teams was obvious. An example appeared in the 9 August 1890 issue of *Sporting Life* in an interesting account of Frank Grant's unpleasant experience, somewhat mollified by a rare (though modest) display of support from his white teammates, when the Harrisburg team of the Atlantic Association boarded at the Clayton House Hotel in Wilmington, Delaware:

> The . . . team was here a few days ago and all the members, including Grant, the Negro player, were quartered at the Clayton. Grant took his meals in the dining room with the rest of the guests, and was assigned a sleeping apartment in the guests' hall. The boarders protested against being obliged to eat in the same dining-room with a colored man, and threatened to leave the house unless the dusky-hued ball player was turned out. Mr. Pyle, however, allowed him to stay with his fellow players while they remained here. This morning the club returned and with them Grant. They applied at the hotel for board, and Proprietor Pyle informed them he would accommodate all but the colored man. The white players determined to stick by their sable-hued companion and all marched out of the hotel in high dudgeon over the refusal to accommodate Grant. Another hotel was sought, where the players were given rooms with the understanding that Grant

must eat with the colored help or get his meals elsewhere. He accepted the latter alternative.

A few teams, as we have seen, such as the Page Fence Giants of the late 1890s and the Chicago American Giants of the early-twentieth century, solved this vexing problem by traveling in a private railroad coach. But such opulence was rare. With the procurement of such mundane necessities as meals, lodging, and transportation becoming so complicated, the black baseball team owner's task became that much more challenging than that of his white counterpart.

THE PROPAGANDA OF SEGREGATION

Propaganda is a terrible thing. The propaganda of segregation and bigotry is evil. It deceives people. I used to have Negroes occasionally tell me, "Do you think Negroes can play in the major leagues?" And do you know what I would say to them? I would say, "Do you think so and so here, who is a barber, can cut hair like a white man?" I would say, "Do you think Doctor so-and-so, who is teaching in a medical school, can teach a white professor?" Well, certainly. And I would say, "What's baseball that I can't play it like a white?" [T]he whole point is that the propaganda of keeping the Negro out of the major leagues made even some of the Negroes think that we didn't have the ability. It started them to thinking it too. – Dave Malarcher, player and manager of the Chicago American Giants in the 1920s [24]

Even worse than the inconvenience brought about by Jim Crow was the imposition on all African Americans, including those in baseball, of a dual personality. For the black American was always utterly aware that he was, simultaneously, both black *and* American – and the two components were not always in harmony. Indeed, in the mind of the white supremacist, the two were mutually exclusive, as expressed by Thomas Dixon in his 1902 novel *The Leopard's Spots*, when he wrote, "who thinks of a Negro when he says 'American'?" [25] James Weldon Johnson in *The Autobiography of an Ex-Coloured Man* describes this dual personality as "the dwarfing, warping, distorting influence which operates upon each and every coloured man in the United States. He is forced to take his outlook on all things, not from the view-point of a citizen, or a man, or even a human being, but from the view-point of a *coloured* man."[26]

W. E. B. DuBois put it more angrily in *The Souls of Black Folk*:

It is a peculiar sensation, this double-consciousness, this sense of always looking at one's self through the eyes of others, of measuring one's soul by the tape of a world that looks on in amused contempt and pity. One ever feels his twoness, – an American, a Negro; two souls, two thoughts, two unreconciled strivings; two warring ideals in one dark body, whose dogged strength alone keeps it from being torn asunder.

The history of the American Negro is the history of this strife, – this longing to attain self-conscious manhood, to merge his double self into a better and truer self. In this merging he wishes neither of the older selves to be lost.... He simply wishes to make it possible for a man to be both a Negro and an American, without being cursed and spit upon by his fellows, without having the doors of Opportunity closed roughly in his face.[27]

In baseball, too, onerous, extraneous demands were placed on African American players for no other reason than their race, unknown baggage to white players. Even in the 1880s, before unrestrained *apartheid* came to prevail, the first rule of survival for the African American player was the clear comprehension that more was expected of him than just his ability. For the African American player, unlike his white compatriot, professional talent was necessary but not sufficient, for he also was expected to contend with hostility and deprivation. All players had to become proficient with bats and balls, but only African Americans were expected to contend with brickbats and blackballs.

Sol White commiserated with the black ballplayer's plight, having known it himself. "In no other profession," he wrote, "has the color line been drawn more rigidly than in base ball" (p. 74). He was clear-eyed about the discouraging prospects of a career in African American baseball. "As it is," he lamented, "the field for the colored professional is limited to a very narrow scope in the base ball world. When he looks into the future he sees no place for him [in the white major leagues]. Consequently, he loses interest. He knows that, so far shall I go, and no further, and, as it is with the profession, so it is with his ability" (p. 118).

WAITING FOR ONE GOOD MAN

In naming a few of the many colored players of Major League calibre, we are not unmindful of those who are yet to come. – Sol White *(p. 118)*

Yet despite the crippling layers of prejudice heaped on African Americans and their baseball, White remained hopeful that one day the barriers would tumble. In the meantime, he urged the black baseball community to prepare themselves to partake of the inevitable blessings of true athletic democracy:

> Base ball is a legitimate profession. As much so as any other vocation, and should be fostered by owners and players alike. . . . It should be taken seriously by the colored player, as honest efforts with his great ability will open an avenue in the near future wherein he may walk hand-in-hand with the opposite race in the greatest of all American games – base ball. (p. 67)

He reported a rumor that an unnamed National League manager wished to break the color line by signing William Clarence Matthews, Harvard University's star shortstop from 1902 through 1905. White most likely was concealing the identity of John J. McGraw, blustery, innovative manager of the New York Giants, who is said to have employed two black stars, Rube Foster and Jose Mendez, known in his native Cuba as "El Diamante Negro" (the Black Diamond), at various times to coach his pitchers. White realized that the time was not yet ripe for mainstream white baseball to accept black players, but, for him, even such historical dead-ends as Matthews's truncated career bred optimism, for "when such actions come to notice there are grounds for hoping that some day the bar will drop and some good man will be chosen from out of the colored profession that will be a credit to all, and pave the way for others to follow" (p. 78). Matthews played in an informal league in Vermont, outside white baseball's organized structure, and even there faced resistance from his fellow players. He abandoned baseball, returned to Harvard, and became a lawyer. White would have to wait another forty years before his "good man," Jackie Robinson, would "pave the way for others to follow."

White's long-term optimism in the face of dire circumstances may have been bolstered by his knowledge, grounded in experience, that black talent had not always been eschewed by white baseball. He was aware, for example, that Stovey, Walker, and the Cuban Giants's Arthur Thomas all had attracted the interest of major-league teams in 1886 and 1887. The Trenton *Daily True American* of 29 June 1886 reported that representatives of the Philadelphia Athletics "were here yesterday endeavoring to engage Thomas, but he declined." The Giants's interest in Stovey for their pennant drive in 1886 is related in chapter 9. On 9 April 1887 the Newark *Daily Journal* reported that Giants manager Jim Mutrie offered to purchase the contracts of both Stovey and Walker, "but [Newark] Manager Hackett informed him they were not on sale." (On p. 76, White says the offer came from John M. Ward, then the team's captain and shortstop.) White may have reasoned that race relations in baseball (and elsewhere) were not static but dynamic and a situation that had deteriorated in the past could improve in the future.

It also may be that White recognized the great truth of racial discrimination: white baseball, in banishing African Americans, was inflicting a wound on itself. Not only were white fans deprived of the joy of watching scores of the greatest baseball players over the many decades, indeed generations, of the Jim Crow era, but white owners were neglecting an ever-growing market of fervid black fans. American baseball would attain its fulfillment only when it cured itself of this disease.

NEITHER GIANTS NOR CUBANS

The Cuban Giants, who, by the way, are neither giants nor Cubans, but thick-set and brawny colored men, make about as stunning an exhibition of ball playing as any team in the country. Old time ball players . . . will have a revival of old memories if they go to see the Cuban Giants when they are really loaded for bear. They play great ball, but, outside of

that they do more talking, yelling, howling and bluffing than all the
teams in the [National] League put together. There is a . . . spirit among
them which carries the spectators back a good many years in ball play-
ing. . . . [I]t is one of the best teams in the city to see. – New York Sun,
quoted in Sporting Life, *5 September 1888*

Despite the occasional minor errors in White's text (typographi-
cal errors have been corrected to the best of the editor's ability in
the current edition), his account of the first twenty years of black
professional baseball has withstood the scrutiny of subsequent historical research. Contemporary coverage, especially in the black
press, pretty much confirms White's version of most events and
testifies to his credibility and reliability as a historian.

One area, however, requires a somewhat closer examination,
namely, his depiction of the birth of African American baseball's
first team of salaried professionals, the Cuban Giants. This team is
of special interest because it was the progenitor of what would
evolve into the Negro Leagues, which was not only a source of pride
and joy among black Americans in the twentieth century but also
one of the most successful African American business enterprises
during the bleak decades of racial exclusion.

Most accounts of the origins of this oddly named team of non-
Cuban nongiants convey two vivid, colorful images, and in doing so,
they recite, as if by rote, White's account. In his *Guide*, White
introduced one element of the commonly told tale when he wrote
that this team was formed in 1885 by Frank Thompson, headwaiter
at the Argyle Hotel in the resort community of Babylon, New York,
from among the African American staff. According to White, this
fortuitous combination of menial hotel employees turned out to be
quite auspicious for Thompson. Breaking free of its Long Island
moorings, the neophyte team took to the road and signed several
key players from the Orions, a strong black semipro team from
Philadelphia. In 1886 they settled in Trenton, New Jersey, and
called themselves the Cuban Giants (pp. 8–10).

The second prevailing image of the team's birth, as well as the
usual explanation of its name, also derives from White, from an

Argyle Hotel, Babylon, N.Y. This 350-room resort, built in 1882, never exceeded one-third capacity and was closed in 1897. Seven years later it was dismantled and the lumber used to build twenty homes on the former hotel grounds. In July 1885 the hotel engaged the Keystone Athletics, an all-black team formed in Philadelphia by hotel headwaiter, Frank P. Thompson, to play games as entertainment for the guests. In August the Athletics merged with the Orions of Philadelphia and the Manhattans of Washington DC to create the Cuban Giants, the first African American all-professional baseball team. Courtesy Village of Babylon Historical and Preservation Society.

interview by Alvin F. Harlow for an article in the September 1938 issue of *Esquire* magazine:

> Most old-timers today are vague as to the origin of [the name Cuban Giants], but Sol White – who joined the club four years later, and may now be seen sauntering about Harlem on pleasant afternoons – says that the version which came to him is that when that first team began playing away from home, they passed as foreigners – Cubans, as they finally decided – hoping to conceal the fact that they were just American Negro hotel waiters,

and talked a gibberish to each other on the field which, they hoped, sounded like Spanish.[28]

How accurate is this picturesque tale, in "the version which came to him," of ballplaying waiters disguised as Cubans, jabbering in mock Spanish to avoid the disapprobation of racist white fans? Is it factual or fanciful, historical or apocryphal, or does it contain elements of both? Can it be that Sol White's story (or parts of it) of the birth of the first black professional baseball team has, as Samuel Johnson said of Shakespeare's histories, every virtue except that of being right?

A different account of the formation of the Cuban Giants appeared in the *New York Age* of 15 October 1887 (reprinted in chapter 4). The *Age*'s Boston correspondent, covering the Cuban Giants's appearance there, wrote that the team was born of a merger of three independent black semipro teams: the Keystone Athletics and the Orions, both of Philadelphia, and the Manhattans of Washington DC. The Keystone Athletics, according to the *Age*, were formed by Frank Thompson in May 1885 and hired as a baseball team by the Argyle that July. Thus, any duties the players performed in Babylon as waiters, bellhops, porters, and the like were incidental to their primary obligation, which was to play baseball for the hotel's guests. The merger with the other two squads, resulting in the creation of the Cuban Giants, took place a month later, in August.

For several reasons, this rendition of events is far more plausible than White's. First, it was written twenty years before White's book and only two years after the fact. Furthermore, the article probably was based on an interview with Thompson himself, who was employed by a Boston hotel at the time. The *Age*'s version of the creation of the Cuban Giants also explains how S. K. Govern came to be the team's first field manager. Govern, a native of the Virgin Islands, had been managing the Manhattans of Washington DC as early as 1882, and some evidence suggests that he had taken that team to play in Cuba during the winter, even before the 1885 alliance that created the Cuban Giants.[29] The Orions's contribution to the tripartite merger (George Williams, Abe Harrison, and Shep Trusty) was even more significant than that of Thompson's Athletics's (Ben Boyd, Ben Holmes, and George Parego), while the Manhattans pitched in with Arthur Thomas and Clarence Williams.

It is doubtful that the team ever attempted to babble in pseudo-Spanish, or if it did so the experiment must certainly have been quickly abandoned. For one thing, it is only remotely conceivable, at best, that nine baseball players could create spontaneous verbal chatter that sounded convincingly like Spanish. More important, not a single press report mentioned it. In fact, before White's statement in *Esquire*, there is no record of anyone, at any time, suggesting that this experiment in linguistic camouflage was ever employed by the team.

African American baseball teams used the name "Giants" with extraordinary frequency well into the twentieth century, in imitation of the National League's extremely successful and popular New York franchise. Referring to black players as "Cubans" was unlikely to deceive many nineteenth-century baseball fans, who were already accustomed to euphemistic references in the sporting press to black players as being "Cuban," "Spanish," or even "Arabian." Still, there may be a kernel of truth to the notion that bookings would be facilitated by implying that this team comprised Cubans rather than African Americans: so much so that nominal subterfuge may indeed explain the choice of the name "Cuban" Giants.

James Weldon Johnson, in his autobiography *Along This Way*, recalled confronting this curious breach in the wall of American racial discrimination during his youth. Johnson, who was raised in Jacksonville, Florida, learned to speak Spanish from a Cuban boyhood friend. On two different occasions while traveling by rail in the 1890s, he noticed that he was treated much better by railroad employees and fellow passengers after they heard him speak Spanish and surmised that he was not African American, but Cuban. "In such situations," Johnson ruefully concluded, "any kind of Negro will do; provided he is not one who is an American citizen."[30]

AVERTING OBLIVION

Without a doubt this record will prove valuable in years to come.
– Pittsburgh Courier, *12 March 1927 (chapter 10)*

The flaws in the details of White's portrayal of the events that led to the birth of the Cuban Giants are attributable to his reliance on secondary accounts. Aside from this lapse, the modern reader can be assured that his work generally is corroborated by recent research. White's literary style, while workmanlike, is hardly redolent of Francis Parkman, or even Moses Fleetwood Walker. But he accomplished his purpose, which was "to follow the mutations of colored base ball, as accurately as possible . . . in the trust that it will meet the approbation of all who may peruse the contents of this book" (p. 3).

Apparently White had some intentions of bringing his story up to date annually, perhaps in the manner of the popular *Reach* and *Spalding Guides* of the era, which chronicled events in white baseball on a yearly basis. The National Baseball Hall of Fame Library, in Cooperstown, New York, has in its possession White's coverage of the 1907 season, written a year after the original book appeared. This supplemental chapter appears in print for the first time in chapter 2, thanks to the assistance of librarian Tom Heitz.

Twenty years after *Sol White's Official Guide: History of Colored Base Ball* was published, White told Floyd J. Calvin of the *Pittsburgh Courier* that he had "a new book he would like to publish, a kind of second edition to his old one, bringing the game from 1907 down to date." The *Courier* passed along to its readers a request to hear from "anyone anywhere in sports circles . . . to help Sol print his record," but no one responded to his call. The same article also reported that "Sol's personal copy of his own book is the only one he knows about and it would be a historical tragedy if this should be lost" (chapter 10).

Nine years later, H. Walter Schlichter, the volume's publisher, was down to two copies of the *Guide* himself, one of which he sent to White at his request. "The other one," he wrote, "I will not part with at any price." He suggested that White try to persuade one of his contacts in the African American press to run an article or series of articles on black baseball history. He informed White that he still had "all the cuts and pictures of the reproductions in the book," and he would gladly supply them to any editor willing to update the *Guide* (chapter 13). However, nothing ever came of this, either.

The historian's pulse quickens at such notions, quixotic as they may be, as that of Schlichter's artwork for Sol White's *Guide* being discovered some lucky day in a long-neglected chest in an attic in Philadelphia. But considering all the ways in which such artifacts as White's account of the birth of black professional baseball can be lost, forgotten, or destroyed over the course of time, one is thankful we still have his history to enable us to examine the past for clues as to what made us what we are. For Sol White's greatest triumph, in a lifetime of devotion to the game he loved so dearly, was the historian's quintessential bounty. To wit, he rescued merit from oblivion.

NOTES

1. Sol White, *Sol White's Official Base Ball Guide: History of Colored Base Ball* (original edition; Philadelphia, 1907), p. 103. Hereinafter cited as *Guide.*

2. Robert W. Peterson, *Only the Ball Was White: A History of Legendary Black Players and All-Black Professional Teams before Black Men Played in the Major Leagues* (Englewood Cliffs, N.J., 1970), p. 30.

3. Cleveland *Gazette*, 29 September 1888.

4. *Sporting Life*, 15 December 1886.

5. *Sporting Life*, 18 May 1887.

6. *Spalding Guide*, 1890, p. 89.

7. Detroit *News*, 10 October 1895.

8. [New York] *Amsterdam News*, 18 December 1930, pp. 149–53.

9. *Guide*, p. 83.

10. *Guide*, p. 101.

11. *Guide*, p. 63.

12. *Guide*, p. 79.

13. *Guide* (original ed.), p. 109.

14. Moses Fleetwood Walker, *Our Home Colony: A Treatise on the Past, Present and Future of the Negro Race in America* (Steubenville, Ohio, 1908), p. 41.

15. Walker, *Our Home Colony*, pp. 26, 30.

16. Walker, *Our Home Colony*, pp. 29, 31.

17. Thomas F. Gossett, *Race: The History of an Idea in America* (Dallas, 1963), p. 271.

18. Gossett, *Race*, p. 253.

19. Sig Synnestvedt, *The White Response to Black Emancipation: Second-Class Citizenship in the United States Since Reconstruction* (New York, 1972), p. 41.

20. Gossett, *Race*, p. 280.

21. Synnestvedt, *White Response*, p. 119.

22. C. Vann Woodward, *The Strange Career of Jim Crow* (2d. rev. ed.; New York, 1966), pp. xii, 26.

23. Woodward, *Strange Career*, p. 33.

24. John Holway, *Voices from the Great Black Baseball Leagues* (New York, 1975), p. 56.

25. Gilbert Osofsky, ed., *The Burden of Race: A Documentary History of Negro-White Relations in America* (New York, 1967), p. 190.

26. James Weldon Johnson, *The Autobiography of an Ex-Coloured Man* (New York, 1960; orig. ed., 1912), p. 21.

27. W. E. B. DuBois, *The Souls of Black Folk* (New York, 1969; orig. ed., 1903), pp. 45–46.

28. Alvan F. Harlow, "Unrecognized Stars," *Esquire*, September 1938, p. 75.

29. *Trenton Times*, 2 July 1886.

30. James Weldon Johnson, *Along This Way* (New York, 1990; orig. ed., 1933), pp. 65, 89.

Every effort has been made to reproduce the original texts faith-
fully. Several editorial changes have silently been made for the
sake of consistency and accuracy, however.

   In the original documents, Sol White's name is variously spelled
"Sol." and "Sol"; in this volume, we have standardized the spelling
to "Sol" throughout. The owner of the Royal Giants of Brooklyn,
John W. Connor, pitcher George Stovey, and right-fielder
Eugene J. "Gabbie" Milliner endured variant spellings of their
names, which we have corrected. The name of the Cuban X-Giants
was also variously written; we have inserted the hyphen where it
was missing. Other names have been corrected, as have dates,
where we have been able to identify the original as being in error.
Finally, on page 18, Lincoln was identified as being in "Nev."; we
have returned it to Nebraska.

1   # SOL WHITE'S

OFFICIAL

BASE BALL GUIDE

by Sol White

Captain, Philadelphia Giants

Champions 1905-1906-1907

Edited by

H. Walter Schlichter

Philadelphia, Pa.

Copyright, 1907 by

H. Walter Schlichter

PREFACE

Since the advent of the colored man in base ball, this is the first book ever published wherein the pages have been given exclusively to the doings of the players and base ball teams.

Realizing the great progress made, and the interest displayed by the players and the public in general, I have endeavored to follow the mutations of colored base ball, as accurately as possible, from the organization of the first colored professional team in 1885, to the present time, in the trust that it will meet the approbation of all who may peruse the contents of this book.

To the players and managers of the past and present and the patrons of colored base ball, to them I dedicate this book.

SOL WHITE

Sol White was born in Bellaire, O., June 12, 1868, and learned to play ball when quite a youngster. When but 16 years of age he attracted the attention of managers of independent teams throughout the Ohio Valley and his services were in great demand. His original position was short stop, but by playing on different teams, he developed into a great all-round player filling any position from catcher to right field.

His first professional engagement was with the Keystones, of Pittsburgh, a member of the Colored League, in 1887. He was assigned to left field and later was placed at second base, where he played brilliantly.

After the Colored League disbanded he was signed by Wheeling, W. Va., of the Ohio League, and assigned to third base. He stood second in batting among the members of his club with an average of .381. In 1888 the color line was drawn in the Ohio League and he played with independent teams during the season.

In 1889 he signed with the Gorhams, of New York, as a catcher, but was assigned to second base where he finished the season.

During 1890 he was a member of the famous York Monarchs, the team that won the pennant in the Pennsylvania League.

In 1891 he joined the "Big Gorhams" composed of former players of the York team.

From 1892 to 1895 he was with the genuine Cuban Giants. 1895 found him with Fort Wayne, Ind., in the Western Inter-State League. The league disbanded in June and he finished the season with the Page Fence Giants, of Adrian, Mich.

After the season of 1895 closed, Sol began a course at Wilberforce University. From 1896 to 1900 he played with the C. X. Giants in the Summer and attended school during the Winter. In 1900 he left school and joined the Columbia Giants of Chicago. In 1901 he played second base and captained the Cuban X-Giants. In 1902 he organized the Philadelphia Giants and has been captain ever since. Under his guidance the Philadelphia Giants have won the championship of the world every year since.

Sol White, captain and first baseman, Philadelphia Giants.

Washington's Manufactory

314 North Broad Street,
PHILADELPHIA, PA.

Bell 'Phone

Washington's Custom Made Shirts,
and Waiters' Supplies.

Also a full line of
Ladies' and Children's Wearing
Apparel; large stock of Side-
combs, Ruching-pins, Collars,
Handkerchiefs, etc.

High-grade Stationery, Finest Per-
fumes, and all kinds of Toilet
Articles.

Washington's manufactory.

No colored ball player has had a wider experience in base ball than Sol, and no ball player has profited by experience greater than he has.

Colored base ball owes a great deal of its popularity of late to his hard, earnest, indefatigable work.

COLORED BASEBALL

Babylon, L.I., has the distinction of being the birth-place of the first professional Colored Base Ball team in the world.

It was at Babylon in 1885 that Frank P. Thompson, head-waiter of the Argyle Hotel, chose the best ball players from among his waiters, and organized a base ball club to play as an attraction for the guests of the hotel. He appointed Ben Holmes, third base and Capt.; A. Randolph, first base; Ben Boyd, second base; Wm. Eggleston, short stop; Guy Day, catcher; Geo. Parego, Frank Harris and R. Mortin, pitchers; Milton Dabney, left field and Chas. Nichols, right field.

They played nine games at Babylon against the strongest teams of New York city and Long Island, winning six, losing two and tieing one.

The calibre of ball displayed by the men, led Thompson to start them on the road as professionals. After the hotel season closed, which was about the middle of September, they left Babylon for Philadelphia.

At this time, there was a team of colored ball players in Philadelphia known as the "Orions" which had been beating every independent team in the vicinity of Philadelphia. The boys from Babylon met them, and took them into camp by a score of 6 to 4.

At this time, the Babylon boys were under the management of John F. Lang (white) of Philadelphia. Mgr. Lang signed at once, three of the best players on the "Orion" team, viz. Geo. Williams, second base and Capt.; Abe Harrison, short stop; and Shep Trusty, pitcher. This move on the part of Lang was one of the most important and valuable acts in the history of colored base ball. It made the boys from Babylon the strongest independent team in the East and the novelty of a team of colored players with that distinction

S. K. Govern, manager of the Original Cuban Giants.

made them a valuable asset, which was taken advantage of by Mr. Walter Cook, of Trenton, N.J.

After defeating the "Orions" they met and defeated Philadelphia's crack white team. This team was composed of such well-known players as, Mike Drennan, Gordon Simpson, Boleau Brill, Montgomery Zinn, Collins and Kelly. The colored boys beat them 10–8.

After several games of small importance, they got a chance to demonstrate to the world that they were not out as a novelty alone. They proved their ability and gained great respect as a baseball team by defeating the Bridgeport, Connecticut, team, champions of the Eastern League, by a score of 5–4. This was the game which by their winning, gave them an advantage which has never been enjoyed by a colored team since their entrance into base ball. Walter Cook a capitalist of Trenton, N.J., became their backer; S. K. Govern (colored) their manager, one of the finest base ball grounds in the country their home and "Cuban Giants" their name.

When Mr. Cook signed his men for the following season of 1886, they were the happiest set of men in the world. As one of them told the writer, not one would have changed his position with the President of the United States.

At that time salaries were according to positions. Mr. Cook gave pitchers and catchers, $18.00 per week and expenses; infielders, $15.00 per week and expenses; outfielders $12.00 per week and expenses.

Eighteen hundred and eighty-six saw the Cuban Giants with a line-up picked from all over the country. With the exception of F. Grant, Walker and Fowler, they had the best the colored base ball world could produce. With Clarence Williams and Arthur Thomas as catchers; Billy White, Shep, Trusty and Geo. Stovey pitchers, they were as strong in battery work as any team in the country. Jack Fry, first base, Geo. Williams, second base, and captain, Ben Holmes, third base, and Abe Harrison, shortstop, composed an infield that was fast, tricky and heady. Boyd, in centre field as a regular, and Billy Whyte in left (very fine fielder in those days), and a catcher in right, composed the outfield. The strongest line-up of the Giants this year would have been; C. Williams, catcher; Stovey or Trusty,

Ben Holmes, captain and third baseman of the first professional colored team, of Babylon, L.I.

pitcher; J. Frye, first base; G. Williams, second base; Holmes, third base; Harrison, shortstop; Whyte, left field; Boyd centre field, and Thomas, right field.

They played better ball, by far, this year than the year previous. Their games attracted the attention of base ball writers all over the country, and the "Cuban Giants" were heralded everywhere as marvels of the base ball world. They were not looked upon by the public as freaks, but they were classed as men of talent. They proved to be very shrewd in detecting the inside work and tricks of their opponents, and later would use them to their own advantage.

They closed the season of '86 with a grand record made against National League and the leading college teams.

Eighteen hundred and eight-seven saw the launching of a League of Colored Base Ball Clubs. The cities represented were Boston, New York, Philadelphia, Baltimore, Washington, Pittsburgh and Louisville.

The great prominence attained by the Cuban Giants, no doubt, led some people to think that colored base ball, patterned after the National League, with a team in every big league city, would draw the same number of people.

With Walter Brown (now deceased), of Pittsburgh, as president, they opened the season. May 1st, the Resolutes of Boston traveled to Louisville, Ky., a distance of over one thousand miles, to play two games and open the season in Louisville. The Gorhams, of New York, jumped to Pittsburgh, over four hundred miles. Washington and Baltimore, with a short jump of forty miles, were no better after the first series financially, than the other teams. With a schedule calling for two games for members of the League at each city, and a small guarantee with a privilege of half the gate receipts, it was little wonder some of the teams failed to appear for their second engagement.

The League, on the whole, was without substantial backing and consequently did not last a week. But the short time of its existence served to bring out the fact that colored ball players of ability were numerous. The teams, with the exception of the Keystones, of Pittsburgh, and the Gorhams, of New York, were composed mostly of home talent, so they were not necessarily compelled to dis-

George Williams, captain and second baseman of the Original Cuban Giants.

band. With reputations as clubs from the defunct Colored League, they proved to be very good drawing cards in different sections of the country. The Keystones and Gorhams, especially distinguished themselves by later defeating the Cuban Giants.

A notable event this year was the great Western trip of the Cuban Giants, playing Cincinnati, Indianapolis, Wheeling and other teams of the West. They were quite successful on their tour, winning from Cincinnati and Indianapolis, both big league teams. Their last game on the Western trip was played at Pittsburgh with the Keystones (colored), which ended in a victory for the Keystones by 3–2. George Miller, catcher of the Pittsburgh National League, was umpire. Frank Miller and Weldy Walker were in the points for the Keystones, and Parego and Williams for the Giants.

In justice to the "Giants," it can be said that they were badly crippled at the time and consequently did not display their true form.

Another notable event of the Cuban Giants this year was their great game with the Champion Detroit team of the National League. Detroit had their big four, Brouthers, Rowe, Richardson and White; also Hanlon, now manager of the Cincinnatis; the famous Fred Dunlap, Ganzel, Lady Baldwin, Sam Thompson and Charley Bennett.

The Giants played this great aggregation, and Champions of the World to a standstill; they losing out by a fluke. With the score 4–2 against them in the eighth inning, the Detroits, by a series of errors, in which luck played a prominent part, managed to forge ahead and win out in the ninth by 6–4. It was a wonderful achievement for the "Giants" to hold a team like the Detroits were at the time down to such a score, as they were considered by all to be the greatest team of sluggers ever gotten together. Too much credit cannot be given Billy Whyte, who pitched for the Cubans, and would have won his game with proper support.

Eighteen hundred and eighty-eight found the Cuban Giants under the management of S. K. Govern and J. M. Bright. Mr. Cook having died during the season of '87.

The Gorhams, of New York, were now the full-fledged rivals of the Cuban Giants in the East. With Nat Collins, John Nelson, An-

William Whyte, pitcher, Original Cuban Giants.

drew Jackson, Frank Pell, Oscar Jackson, John Evans, Bob Jackson, Vactor and Davis, they were making a great record throughout New York, New Jersey and Connecticut. They beat the Cuban Giants in Newburgh, N.Y., 4-3.

The important event of this year was the base ball tournament held in New York. The prize a silver ball, was donated by J. M. Bright, part owner of the Cuban Giants. The following clubs entered: Cuban Giants, Keystones of Pittsburgh; Gorhams of New York and the Red Stockings of Norfolk, Va. The teams finished in the order named above. The Cuban Giants winning the ball.

The surprise of the meet was the playing of the Keystones. Their only defeats were at the hands of the Cuban Giants; they won every game played with the Gorhams and Red Sox. The Keystones at this time were not professionals. They having one man other than home talent.

The Red Stockings of Norfolk showed up well in the tournament, but luck seemed to be against them.

All their games were hotly contested, but in the closing innings, luck would invariably step in and beat them.

Eighteen hundred and eighty-nine was an important year in colored base ball. The Cuban Giants, with Harrisburg, Norristown, Lebanon, Lancaster, York, Hazleton and the Gorhams, of New York, formed the Pennsylvania League.

While the Cuban Giants and Harrisburg were fighting for the Championship and running neck and neck, the Gorhams were not out of the running by any means. Harrisburg and the Cuban Giants were much surprised and disconcerted during the season by having two straight defeats registered against them at the hands of the colored boys from New York. The fight for the pennant was bitterly contested between the Harrisburg and Giants. When the last game was played, both teams claimed the pennant. Later it was decided in favor of Harrisburg by a few points.

The intense rivalry between the Cubes and Harrisburg in 1889 led to the formation of the Pennsylvania League the next year on a much stronger basis in every particular. A party of gentlemen who backed the Harrisburg of '89 secured the grounds in York, and signing the Cuban Giants placed them in York as representatives of

Clarence Williams, catcher, Original Cuban Giants.

the League. The same bitter rivalry was carried through the Winter into the season of '90 by partisans of the two teams and when the boys reported in the Spring, they found two of their number missing. To weaken the "Giants" chances for the pennant and to enhance their own, the Harrisburg management had signed C. Williams and F. Grant, of the Cubans. The case of Grant was carried to court as both teams claimed his services for 1890.

The Court decided in favor of Harrisburg. The York management at once signed A. and O. Jackson and White, of the Gorhams. It was quite a race for the lead the first month between York, Harrisburg and Altoona; after which the colored boys gradually pulled away until July, when they were so far in the lead that Harrisburg jumped to the Atlantic League to save them the shame of being left so far behind in a race for the pennant.

It can be said for the management of the Harrisburgs, that although fighting the colored team by every conceivable manner on the ball field, they never drew the color line in any of the League meetings. They would not enter unless their colored player, Frank Grant, was allowed to play.

After the Pennsylvania League disbanded July 5th, the Yorks, colored Monarchs of the Diamond, as J. Monroe Krider, their Mgr. called them, started on a tour of Pennsylvania playing independent ball until the close of the season. While the original Cuban Giants were playing in York, under new management, J. M. Bright, with a team of new material, was playing under the name of Cuban Giants and doing well. It was also during this year that the first colored professional team in the West was started. They were organized in Lincoln, Nebraska, and were called the Lincoln Giants. They had such well-known players as Patterson, now of the Royal Giants; Taylor of Chicago Unions, Miller of the Royal Giants, Maupin, Castone, Reeves, Hughbanks, Lincoln and others.

The Lincoln Giants made a great record during the season of 1890 playing Western League and State League teams: but their backing was not strong enough for a continuance in the business and 1890 saw the last of the Lincoln Giants.

The Lincoln Giants were strong in batteries, hard hitters and fast

George Parago, pitcher, Original Cuban Giants.

runners. They were hard to beat unless a strong pitcher was against them.

There were no other colored professional teams at this time except the Colored Monarchs of York (formerly players of original Cuban Giants); Cuban Giants, J. M. Bright, mgr.; Gorhams, of New York, A. Davis, mgr. Up to this time there is no record of any other strictly professional colored teams. This year saw the close of a period in colored base ball which may well be called the money period. From 1885 until the close of 1890, colored base ball flourished. The causes for the change in the condition of things are commented upon in another part of this book.

Eighteen hundred and ninety-one saw quite a change in the line-up by the colored teams of the East. A. Davis, proprietor of the Gorhams, signed every man of the York Monarchs. In addition, he signed C. Williams, F. Grant and Geo. Stovey. This team, now known as the Big Gorhams, was without a doubt one of the strongest teams ever gotten together, white or black. Their ages ranging from 22 to 32; every man placed where he was strongest, pitchers and catchers strong in field and at bat, every man a student of the game and experienced, they were a hard team for any club to beat. Their line-up was as follows: Arthur Thomas and Clarence Williams, catchers; Geo. Stovey, Wm. Selden and W. Malone, pitchers; Geo. Williams, first base; Sol White, second base; A. Jackson, third base; F. Grant, short stop; O. Jackson, centre field, and pitchers or catchers in left and right fields.

This year marked the decline of colored base ball in the East for several years. The Lincoln Giants did not reorganize in 1891 their players getting on with white teams in Nebraska and other points in the West.

The Big Gorhams made a record never equaled by any colored team. They played over one hundred games and lost four. They won thirty-nine straight games. New Brunswick beat them the first game, University of Vermont the second, over a month later Glens Falls won from them, and the last was a colored team called the Little Gorhams under the same management as the Big Gorhams.

During this season of 1892 there was only one colored team in

Arthur Thomas (deceased), catcher, Original Cuban Giants.

William Malone, pitcher, Original Cuban Giants.

Benj. Boyd, center fielder, Original Cuban Giants.

the East, the Cuban Giants under the management of J. M. Bright. The season of '91 was so disastrous financially that the Big Gorhams did not re-organize in '92.

While amateur base ball was flourishing in the West, there was no colored professional teams since the Lincoln Giants disbanded, and 1893 and 1894 still saw the one team in the East, the Cuban Giants, although Boston tried for it for a while in '93 but the team only lasted a month.

In 1895 conditions became more encouraging in the East and West, a difference between manager and players of the Cuban Giants. In this year the second colored professional team was organized in the West. It was Grant Johnson in connection with Bud Fowler who conceived the idea of a colored team traveling in a private car and giving street parades on bicycles prior to every game. Grant and Bud found substantial backing for their project in the persons of Messrs Hock, Taylor and Parsons of Adrian, Mich., and in 1895 a new team was launched from whence graduated some of the best colored players of the present time.

With Grant Johnson as Capt. and "Malone," an old Cuban Giant player to steady the youngsters, Johnson and Fowler selected a team of unknown players who made a great record. The private car and bicycles were good advertisements. The team was known as the Page Fence Giants.

The Page Fence Giants was a fine base ball team. They were hard to beat in '95 as their pitchers were among the best and their fielding excellent. With Johnson, Fowler, Patterson, Burns, Brooks, Taylor, Holland, Malone, White, Vandyke, Binga and Miller, the Giants of Adrian were formidable opponents to any team.

In this year can be recorded the first fatality on the ball field in connection with colored base ball. During a game in Hastings, Mich., Brooks, centre fielder of the Page Fence Giants dropped while running after a fly ball and never recovered consciousness. He died within an hour. Owing to the weakness of the teams in Michigan and Northern Ohio and the great strength of the Page Fence Giants they (the Giants) had easy sailing during the season and won as they pleased.

The "Chicago Unions" had been the leading amateur colored

John Frye (deceased), first baseman, Original Cuban Giants.

team of the West since 1886 and during the spring of 1896 they organized to play Sunday games only, with the prairie teams of the city of Chicago. They won every game played during the first season against all kinds of odds, the umpires and crowds in general being against them. Nevertheless they won out and closed the season with a clear record of victories.

They continued playing on the prairies until 1891 when they secured a small ground at 67th street and Langley avenue, playing Sunday games only upon them. They had quite a success for several seasons.

The spring of 1894 found them at 37th and Butler streets where they were more centrally located.

Up to the season of 1896, the team played as amateurs only playing the crack amateur clubs of Chicago, but during 1896 under the management of Messrs. Peters and Leland they branched out as an independent professional team playing every Sunday in Chicago and during the week touring the States of Indiana, Illinois, Wisconsin, Michigan and Iowa: meeting all the professional organizations throughout that county.

Summing up the records of the club during the first twelve seasons of its existence, they made an enviable record by playing 731 games. They won 613 and lost 118 and tied 12 which gave them a percentage of .814 for the twelve years.

For the last few years the Unions have been under the management of W. S. Peters, F. Leland having organized the Leland Giants of Chicago.

The Unions have given to the base ball world some of the best ball players in the profession. In the early years of the Unions, "Hopkins," a pitcher was the star of the West, but later gave away to Holland, Buckner, Horn and other ambitious youngsters who are still in the game and doing fine work.

The Unions have produced such players as Hyde, Moore, Holland, Buckner, Horn, Monroe, Jones, Wyatt, Barton and others of note in the colored profession.

The Unions have always been hard hitters and good fielders. Their fault seemed to lie in the lack of interest taken in the fine points of the game.

Harry Johnson, utility man, Original Cuban Giants.

With their hitting and fielding ability coupled with speed on the bases they would have been unbeatable.

In the East there was a new team called the Cuban X-Giants, under the management of E. B. Lamar, Jr., of New York.

Colored base ball was again at a stand-still in the East and there was nothing of importance to chronicle until 1899. Then came the trip of the Cuban X-Giants in 1897 when they played Chicago, St. Louis, Louisville and Cincinnati. That was the longest trip ever taken by any colored club in America.

In 1899 the Page Fence Giants of Adrian, Michigan, were stationed in Chicago at Thirty-ninth and Wentworth avenue. They were then called the Columbia Giants and were under the management of John W. Patterson. The Columbia Giants with their additional pitcher, Buckner, from the Chicago Unions, were stronger in points at that time than any other colored team. Wilson, Miller, and Buckner formed a trio of twirlers hard to duplicate. Burns and Johnson, catchers; Johnson, Jr., first base; C. Grant, second base; B. Binga third base; G. Johnson, short stop; and Captain Patterson, left field; Barton, centre field, and Reynolds right field. The "Giants" started with good substantial backing having behind them the Columbia Club, an organization composed of Chicago's best business and professional men. Their grounds at Thirty-ninth street and Wentworth avenue were nicely located and their uniforms consisting of a traveling uniform of gray material and a home uniform of white were of the finest. Of the Columbia Giants, it can be said, they were the finest and best equipped colored team that was ever in the business.

The Columbia Giants in opposition to the Unions drew well on Sundays, but their games away from home were not successful financially. In this year there were the Cuban X-Giants and Genuine Cuban Giants in the East, the Red Stockings of Norfolk, Va. in the South and the Chicago Unions and Columbia Giants in the West. Five colored professional base ball teams.

The same teams were still in existence in 1900. Nothing of importance happening in colored base ball this year. The teams of the East were doing well financially while in the West, the teams were holding their own.

John M. Bright, manager, Genuine Cuban Giants.

"Pop" Watkins, captain and original coacher, Genuine Cuban Giants.

Nineteen hundred and one saw quite a change in Western base ball circles, the facts of which are chronicled in another part of this book.

In 1902 the Philadelphia Giants, the present Colored Champions, were organized. Harry Smith, base ball writer of the Philadelphia Tribune, conceived the idea of a professional team to represent Philadelphia. So he, in connection with H. Walter Schlichter, of the Philadelphia Item, and the writer, organized the team which are known as the Colored World's Champions. The team as then composed was as follows: Clarence Williams, c.; Wm. Bell, Chas. (Kid) Carter, and John Nelson, pitchers; Harry Smith, first base; Frank Grant, second base; Sol White, short stop; John Hill, third base; Andrew Payne, left field; John Manning, centre field. Like any team during their first year, the changes in their line-up were many, but they played good ball and were very popular.

From 1903 until 1906 there was nothing of importance occurring, other than championship contests, which are noted in another part of the book.

In 1906 a new team appeared in the field. J. W. Connor, colored, of Brooklyn, owner of the Royal Cafe, organized a team and called them the Royal Giants. They are now managed and captained by Grant Johnson, of Page Fence and Columbia Giants fame, and they are now one of the leading colored clubs of the country.

The year of 1906 was notable in colored base ball circles. There seemed to be a base ball epidemic, especially in the East. Within a radius of one hundred miles there was no less than nine professional colored base ball teams. viz.: Philadelphia Giants, Cuban X-Giants, Genuine Cuban Giants, Royal Giants, Quaker Giants of N.Y., Wilmington Giants, New York Giants, Baltimore Giants, of Newark and Keystone Giants, of Philadelphia. There were also two teams from Cuba: Cuban Stars and Havana Stars. With the forming of the International League, some of the teams managed to last until after the Fourth of July. The Quaker Giants, Wilmington Giants and Havana team disbanded in the latter part of July.

The season ended with the Philadelphia Giants, Cuban X-Giants, Royal Giants and Genuine Giants battling for supremacy in the East, and the Chicago Unions and Leland Giants in the West. The Royal

A. Garcia (deceased), Genuine Cuban Giants.

Giants, of Brooklyn were considerably strengthened by the addition of Patterson, Johnson, Jr., Monroe and Wright, of the defunct Quaker Giants. The Cuban X-Giants, with Buckner and Barton, of the Quaker Giants, and Gatewood and Petway, of the Leland Giants of Chicago, were far stronger at the close of the season than in the beginning. The Cuban Giants added Earl, a pitcher, to their line-up, and the "Phillies" grabbed Francis, third baseman of the defunct Wilmington Giants.

The International League, with Freihoffer, president, and John A. O'Rourke, secretary, organized with the following members: Cuban X-Giants, Quaker Giants, of New York; Cuban Stars, Havanas, of Cuba; Philadelphia Professionals and Riverton-Palmyra Athletics. Later the Wilmington Giants took the place of one of the Cuban teams, and the Philadelphia Giants joined the League in August, taking the place of the Quaker Giants.

The Philadelphia Giants won the pennant and a beautiful cup donated by President Freihoffer. The deciding game was played on the American League grounds, Philadelphia, September 3d, Labor Day, before 10,000 people, the largest crowd of spectators that ever attended a base ball game between colored teams.

This virtually ended the season of colored base ball and settled the question of premiership among the teams of the East and the West also.

The Philadelphia Giants, by the hardest struggle of their career, still maintained the name of World's Colored Champion by winning a majority of games played with every colored team in the East and winning also from the Chicago Unions and Leland Giants of the West. By playing three games in one day and winning all they established a wonderful record. On September 30th they met the Royal Giants in a morning game at Elizabeth, N.J., and defeated them 6–1. In the afternoon they met the Cuban X-Giants at Brighton Oval, Brooklyn, and defeated them 5–2, and later in the day played Brighton Athletic Club and beat them 6–2. This day, September 30th, marked the close of twenty years of professional Colored Base Ball. Taking lessons from the past, there seems to be nothing but the brightest prospects for great advancement in the future.

Chase Lyons, pitcher, Genuine Cuban Giants.

Championship contests of a local nature are as a rule more bitterly fought than others of a different character. There will not be found the same feeling displayed during a contest when the teams are from distant parts of the country as when there is a local contest.

When teams travel to a far section of the country to meet for a championship struggle, there is always given to the visitors a most hearty welcome. With a friendly grasp of the hand and a "Pleased to meet you" and a "I hope we will have a good game," style of greeting, they are escorted to their hotel by the home manager and self appointed committees of "fans" who desire to show visitors a good time while they are in the city. The same good cheer and friendship is carried on the field and while the games are invariably well contested and interesting, they lack that never-say-die spirit that always creeps into a struggle between teams of the same section of the country, or two teams battling for prestige in an immediate locality.

Situations, as described above, occur yearly in colored base ball. East and West, and go far to keep up the interest among colored patrons of the National game.

The first bitter struggle between colored rivals in the base ball world occurred in 1887. The Cuban Giants, of Trenton, and the Gorhams, of New York, were the first colored teams to clash on the diamond for what may be termed local supremacy. Although located in and around New York, they played to large and appreciative crowds. Their success financially and from a playing sense was phenomenal. The Gorhams, undaunted, hooked up with the Cuban Giants at every opportunity and by hard earnest endeavor played them to a standstill upon all occasions, until at last victory crowned their efforts.

It was at Newburgh, N.Y., when after many futile efforts to gain a victory over the "Giants" the Gorhams, by main grit and nervy ball playing managed to win out in a game replete with sensational fielding and daring acts on the bases. With Nelson and B. Jackson of the Gorhams, opposed to Parego and Williams for the Giants, the

Cuban X-Giants, season, 1905.

game was bitterly contested until the last inning, when O. Jackson of the Gorhams scored the winning run on an infield hit by mixing it up with Williams at the plate, Williams dropping the ball. The score was 4 to 3.

In 1888 the games played by the Cuban Giants, Keystones of Pittsburgh, Gorhams of New York and Red stockings of Norfolk, for the silver ball and the colored Championship has been fully commented upon in the first part of the book.

In 1889 the Gorhams and Cuban Giants, both members of the Pennsylvania League, played regular league schedule games. At Easton, Pa., the home of the Gorhams, the Giants and Gorhams met to play their first league series of the season.

These games were hotly contested. Malone and Whyte pitched for the Giants; Miller and Nelson for the Gorhams. The series went to the Gorhams, they won both games by the same score, 4-3.

There were no other championship games between colored

teams until 1896 when the Cuban X-Giants went West to play the Page Fence Giants, of Adrian, Michigan. (Although in 1894, the Cuban Giants took their first trip west to play the Chicago Unions, the two games played were of minor importance as the Unions at that time were amateurs and somewhat easy for the Giants.) The colored championship was not involved in this contest between the Cuban X-Giants and the Page Fence Giants, as the Cuban X-Giants had never met the Genuine Cuban Giants of the East nor had the Page Fence Giants met the Chicago Unions of the West, but the games were played as though the world's premiership rested on the outcome. The agreement called for fifteen games. The team winning eight games of the fifteen to be declared winner of the series and a championship. The Page Fence Giants, after the second game of the series, won as they pleased. The Cuban X-Giants lacked condition, and after the second game were as bad, physically, as a team in spring practice. The boys from Adrian were in the pink of condition and played great ball. Of the first fifteen games played the Page Fence Giants won ten and the Cuban X-Giants five.

The Page Fence Giants were given beautiful medals by their manager and also an extra compensation for winning the series.

The first championship games in the East since the Cuban Giant – Gorham struggle took place at the Weehauken grounds in the fall of 1897 between the Genuine Cuban Giants and the Cuban X-Giants. The games were played three successive Sundays and resulted in two out of three for the Cuban X-Giants which gave them undisputed right to the Colored Championship of the East.

In 1899 the first real championship games between the East and West were played. The Cuban X-Giants the real colored champions of the East journeyed to Chicago to play a series of games with the "Unions" of Chicago. The "Unions" were stronger this year than at any time since their organization. Footes, Jackson, Horn, Holland, Moore, Hopkins, Hyde, Monroe, W. Jones and Bert Jones were the men that composed the Unions. The Cuban X-Giants had Williams, Selden, Nelson, Howard, Wilson, F. Grant, A. Jackson, White, W. Jackson and Jordan. Fourteen games were played in and around Chicago, the crowds on several occasions being enormous.

The games were hotly contested all through the series but the superior hitting of the Cuban X-Giants won for them the title of Champions. They won nine of fourteen games played.

It was in this year that the Page Fence Giants of Adrian, Mich., moved to Chicago and played under the name of the Columbia Giants. While Cuban X-Giants and Unions were playing their series, the Columbia Giants were issuing all sorts of challenges to the winner or the loser. The result was the acceptance by the Unions and the Cuban X-Giants also.

The Union and Columbia Giants had long been at loggerheads owing to the invasion of Chicago by the Page Fence Giants and the Unions heretofore would not entertain a proposition relating to a series with the Giants, out of consideration for the public, the Unions agreed to play a series of five games for the local championship. The Columbia Giants, by their long string of victories during the season were favorites in the betting at ten to seven. The Unions were not without a following and were backed heavily at the prevailing odds. The rivalry was intense and spectators and players were worked to a high pitch of excitement.

The Columbia Giants were stronger in the box than the Unions and made less errors in their fielding. These qualifications won for the Columbia Giants the local Championship of Chicago and a big bunch of money. Of the five games played, the "Unions" did not win a game.

The Columbia Giants now turned their attention to the Cuban X-Giants, of New York. A series of games was arranged between the two teams and was played in Chicago and in towns in Michigan. Eleven games were played. The Cuban X-Giants won the series by seven to four.

Nineteen hundred was a great year for the two Western clubs from a playing standpoint. The Cuban X-Giants, who had been winning from the Unions so consistently year after year, made their annual trip to Chicago for another series with the same team. The Unions won from the "Giants" for the first time in their career. While the Unions were thrashing the Cuban X-Giants, of New York, the Columbia Giants were walloping the Genuine Cuban Giants, of New York.

E. B. Lamar Jr., manager and owner, Cuban X-Giants.

The two Western teams won as they pleased this year.

During two season's following, 1901 and 1902, there were no championship contests in the colored professional ranks.

In nineteen hundred and three, there was the Algona Brownies, of Algona, Ia., a team composed of former Unions and Columbia Giant players, playing the Unions for the championship of the West and the Giants, of Philadelphia, playing the Cuban X-Giants for the premiership of the East.

The Algona Brownies with Geo. Johnson, B. Jones, Horn, Ball, Moore and other noted players, beat the Unions in a series of games which were noted for lack of enthusiasm.

The Philadelphia Giants and the Cuban X-Giants, after two years of squabbling, challenges and counter challenges, got together and arranged to play for the colored championship of the world.

These games were of the utmost importance and were fought with the bitterest feeling at every stage of the series. Eight games were to have been played but the Cuban X-Giants won five of the first seven, thereby winning the championship.

It would have been a hard matter to pick the winner before the series, especially by form in previous games or by the lineup of the nines. Both were strong in the pitching department and good with the stick. The Philadelphia Giants were confident of winning as they had some of the hardest hitters of the colored profession in Robert Footes, William Bell, Charles Carter, Harry Buckner, Sol White, Frank Grant, William Monroe, William Binga, John Patterson, John Nelson and William Evans but the pitching of Foster backed by the superior work of his team-mates won a clean cut victory for the Cuban X-Giants.

The winning team was composed of the following players: Clarence Williams, Robert Jordan, Andrew Foster, Dan McClellan, James Robinson, Ed Wilson, Ray Wilson, Charles Grant, John Hill, Grant Johnson, William Jackson, Andrew Payne and William Smith.

Of the games played Foster won four, McClellan one, Carter one, and Bell one.

The Phillies were out-played in all departments of the game and did not show the form which they displayed in the earlier part of the season.

Ray Wilson, captain, Cuban X-Giants.

John Nelson, pitcher, Cuban X-Giants, 1896–1902.

The features of this contest were the pitching of Foster, who won every game he pitched (four), and the great hitting of Jordan, who hit at a .560 clip during the series.

In 1904, the Cuban X-Giants and Philadelphia Giants again hooked up in another struggle for the Championship. The Phillies, owing to dissension in the team in 1903, were far from being satisfied with their defeat of that year and claimed that with proper

John Hill, shortstop, Cuban X-Giants.

harmony in their ranks, they could turn the trick on their much hated rivals.

This Championship series consisted of three games, which were played in Atlantic City. Both players and spectators were worked to the highest pitch of excitement. Never in the annals of colored baseball did two nines fight for supremacy as these teams fought.

Everything known to baseball was done by both nines to win, but the Phillies by the nerviest kind of ball playing, and the best kind of pitching by Foster, who was now with the Phillies, won two out of three and the proud title of Colored Champions of the World.

The Philadelphia Giants, on paper, seemed to be outclassed when matched with the Cuban X-Giants this season. Below is the personnel of the teams that met in Atlantic City:

Phila. Giants		Cuban X-Giants
R. Footes	Catcher	C. Williams
G. Johnson, Jr.	Catcher	R. Jordan
A. Foster	Pitcher	D. McClellan
C. Carter	Pitcher	A. Ball
W. Bell	Pitcher	J. Robinson
W. Horn	Pitcher	H. Buckner
S. White	First Base	R. Jordan
C. Grant	Second Base	J. Patterson
W. Monroe	Shortstop	G. H. R. Johnson
J. Hill	Third Base	J. Smith
P. Hill	Left Field	W. Jackson
A. Payne	Centre Field	H. Moore
W. Bell	Right Field	W. Smith

In stick work the Philadelphia Giants were supposed to be weak. The Cuban X-Giants were outbattled by fifty-seven points. The Phillies having an average of .201 and the Cubans .144. The Philadelphia Giants played a better fielding game. Their fielding average for the series being .944 while the Cubes' average was .918.

The Cubes stole the most bases, they having seven to their credit, while the Phillies stole five.

W. S. Peters, owner and manager, Chicago Unions.

Patterson and Grant Johnson did the hitting for the Cuban X-Giants. Patterson leading with an average of .346.

Foster in two games led the Phillies with an average of .400. He was followed by Geo. Johnson with .352.

The features of this contest was the pitching of Foster, who pitched two of the three games, winning both and striking out eighteen men in the first game and letting the Cubes down with two hits the third game, the hitting and base running of Patterson, he making two home runs during the series and stealing four bases in one game.

The Philadelphia Giants beat the All-Cubans, of Cuba, three of five games this year, which gave them the title of Champions of Cuba.

In 1905 the colored teams of the East could not come to any agreement, and no series of any kind were arranged.

In the West, the Chicago Union Giants and the Leland Giants were having a battle royal in Chicago for the Championship of the West.

The Union Giants, with Geo. Wilson and Geo. Johnson of the Renville, Minn., team as a battery managed to tie the Leland Giants in the fifth game of the contest, which left the series standing even at two and two.

During 1906 there was a four-cornered fight between the Philadelphia Giants, Cuban X-Giants, and Royal Giants, of Brooklyn, and Wilmington Giants, for the honors of the colored base ball world. The result of the games played left no doubt as to where the honor belonged. The Philadelphia Giants though badly crippled the entire season, won a majority of games from every colored team they played and clearly demonstrated their superiority over all competitors for colored base ball supremacy.

Of the five games played with the Wilmington Giants, the Philadelphia Giants won four and tied one, the Royal Giants of Brooklyn and the Phillies, played seventeen games, the Phillies won eleven and lost six. Of the fifteen games played with the Cuban X-Giants, the Phillies won ten and lost five, making a total of 37 games played by the Phillies against the colored teams of which they won 25, lost

Harry Hyde, captain, Chicago Unions.

David Wyatt, outfielder, Chicago Unions.

11 and tied one, giving them a percentage of .694 against .306 for their opponents.

The success of the Philadelphia Giants of 1906 was due no doubt, to their gameness. A gamer gang of ball players never stepped on a diamond. More or less crippled throughout the season, they played the hardest teams with the same spirit as the weak ones. When the other teams were strengthening by adding stars to their lineup, the Phillies were weakening by accidents and sickness. When the odds against them were greatest, they seemed the more determined and their nonchalant air bred a personality that told their opponents they would have to play ball or they could not win.

The following defy was sent to the winner of the world's series between the Athletics and New Yorks, by Manager Schlichter, of the Philadelphia Giants, through the New York press.

WANTS TO MATCH THE GIANTS FOR THE CHAMPIONSHIP

Walter Schlichter, the well known sporting editor of the "Item," who is also the manager of the Philadelphia Giants, the colored base ball team, is out with a very novel proposition and one that will no doubt startle the whole base ball world. Slick (everybody calls him Slick) took hold of the bunch of colored ball players a couple of years ago and by continually weeding them out and introducing new blood he has made them one of the strongest, wide awake ball teams in the country. Slick has also shown his ability as a press agent and booster by continually advertising the team till they are now known to everyone who takes even the slightest interest in baseball. This has made the Philadelphia Giants one of the best cards in baseball and there is a constant demand for their services seven days a week.

The Philadelphia Giants have won their way to the top and are now the recognized champion colored ball team of the world. Now Schlichter shows that he is ambitious, for he wants to match his team against the winners of the white championship, be it either in the National or the American league. Schlichter wants to play a series of three or five games and thus decide who can play base ball the best – the white or the black American.

At first glance it might seem as if Schlichter's only idea was with the view of making money and that it was not to be taken seriously.

Robert Jackson, catcher, Chicago Unions.

But a careful investigation of the playing record of the Philadelphia Giants will show that they have earned the right to play against the best white teams for they can put an article of base ball that is as good as the best and at any stage of the game they could make either the Athletics or the New York National Leaguers, hustle to win out. Of course, there is a possibility of the colored men winning and that would be distasteful to many followers of the white team, but true sport recognizes no color nor clan and it should always be, may the best man win.

It is to be hoped for the sake of the sport that Schlichter's challenge for a series of games will be accepted by the winners of the white championship. Such a series of games played in Philadelphia and New York would prove a tremendous attraction and be well worth the trouble, for it would mean a big gate for the club owners and a nice wad of money for the players. Here's luck to Slick and hoping that he can get on his championship series.

NOTABLE FEATS
OF COLORED PITCHERS

Of the great feats performed by colored pitchers the game in which Billy Whyte, of the Original Cuban Giants, twirled against the famous Detroit team of 1887, was one of the most noteworthy. Whyte was unexpectedly called upon to face the greatest team of sluggers in the history of the game, and for a time had them at his mercy. Detroit won out in the last two innings by the ragged fielding of the Giants. Whyte was one of the best colored pitchers the game ever saw. Below is the score by innings of the Cuban Giants-Detroit game of 1887:

									R.	H.	E.
Detroit	0	0	1	0	1	0	0	2	2 – 6	6	0
Cuban Giants	0	1	0	2	0	0	1	0	0 – 4	8	4

Batteries—Conway and Ganzel for Detroit; Whyte and Williams for Cuban Giants.

"The Roadside"

514 S. 15th Street
PHILADELPHIA, PENNA.

"The Roadside."

"The Item."

George Stovey struck out twenty-two of the Bridgeport (Conn.) Eastern League team in 1886 and lost his game.

Dan McClellan, of the Philadelphia Giants, is the only pitcher of color who has the distinction of blanking a team without a hit or run or a man reaching first. McClellan accompanied this feat against the York, Pa., team in 1903.

York, Pa., July 17–Before McClellan's masterly pitching the Penn Park Athletic Club today was shut out without a single player reaching first base and only 27 batting in the game.

										R.	H.	E.
Penn Park	0	0	0	0	0	0	0	0	0 – 0	0	4
Cuban X-Giants ...	0	0	0	2	3	0	0	0	x – 5	12	6

Batteries–Hilbert and Smith; McClellan and Williams. Umpire– Sturgen. Time, 1.05. Attendance, 600.

McClellan pitched a great game in 1905 against the Newark Eastern League team keeping hits well scattered and shutting them out 4 to 0.

NEWARK

	AB.	R.	H.	O.	A.	E.
Cockman, 3b	4	0	3	2	2	0
Murphy, cf	3	0	0	1	0	0
Jons, lf	3	0	1	4	0	0
Dillard, rf	3	0	1	0	0	0
Gatins, ss	4	0	0	3	6	2
Connors, 1b	4	0	1	11	1	0
Mahling, 2b	4	0	1	2	2	0
Latimer, c	4	0	1	3	1	0
McPherson, p	4	0	0	1	3	2
*Skopec	1	0	0	0	0	0
Totals	34	0	8	27	15	4

*Batted for McPherson in ninth.

Red Stockings, of Norfolk, Va., season, 1904.

PHILADELPHIA GIANTS

	AB.	R.	H.	O.	A.	E.
Grant, 2b	4	1	0	5	3	0
Hill, lf	4	1	2	4	0	0
Monroe, 3b	4	1	1	2	1	0
Johnson, ss	3	1	0	2	7	0
Moore, cf	4	0	2	2	0	0
McClellan, p	4	0	0	0	1	0
Foster, rf	4	0	0	0	0	0
White, 1b	4	0	0	8	0	0
Devoe, c	3	0	0	4	0	0
Totals	34	4	5	27	12	0

Newarks .... 0 0 0 0 0 0 0 0 0 – 0
Phila. Giants .... 1 0 3 0 0 0 0 0 0 – 4

Batteries–McPherson and Latimer. McClellan and Devoe. Umpire, Mr. Snyder.

Foster, of the Philadelphia Giants, from his consistent work of

NEWARK.

	AB.	R.	H.	O.	A.	E.
Cockman, 3b	4	0	3	2	2	0
Murphy, cf	3	0	0	1	0	0
Jons, lf	3	0	1	4	0	0
Dillard, rf	3	0	1	0	0	0
Gatins, ss	4	0	0	3	6	2
Connors, 1b	4	0	1	11	1	0
Mahling, 2b	4	0	1	2	2	0
Latimer, c	4	0	1	3	1	0
McPherson, p	4	0	0	1	3	2
*Skopec	1	0	0	0	0	0
Totals	34	0	8	27	15	4

*Batted for McPherson in ninth.

PHILADELPHIA GIANTS.

	AB.	R.	H.	O.	A.	E.
Grant, 2b	4	1	0	5	3	0
Hill, lf	4	1	2	4	0	0
Monroe, 3b	4	1	1	2	1	0
Johnson, ss	3	1	0	2	7	0
Moore, cf	4	0	2	2	0	0
McClellan, p	4	0	0	0	1	0
Foster, rf	4	0	0	0	0	0
White, 1b	4	0	0	8	0	0
Devoe, c	3	0	0	4	0	0
Totals	34	4	5	27	12	0

```
Newarks  .. ....0 0 0 0 0 0 0 0 0—0
Phila. Giants ..1 0 3 0 0 0 0 0 0—4
```

Batteries—McPherson and Latimer; McClellan and Devoe. Umpire, Mr. Snyder.

Foster, of the Philadelphia Giants, from his consistant work of the past four seasons, has earned the reputation of being one of the best colored pitchers the game has produced.

Foster has pitched several no hits

Boxscore of 1906 Newark (Eastern League)–Philadelphia Giants game, reproduced from the original edition of White's Guide.

Kimball's
Anti-Rheumatic
Ring

A speedy and permanent cure for rheumatism, neuralgia, sciatica gout, paralysis and all other diseases where a general warming quickening, strengthening and equalization of the circulation is required.

———

Kimball's Anti-Rheumatic Ring.

the past four seasons, has earned the reputation of being one of the best colored pitchers the game has produced.

Foster has pitched several no hits games, and has struck out as high as 18 men in a single game against such teams as the Trenton Y.M.C.A. of 1904 and the Cuban X-Giants of 1904.

Below is the tabulated scores of three games in which Foster's work was remarkable.

CAMDEN

	R.	H.	O.	A.	E.
Meehan, cf	0	0	2	0	0
Miller, c	0	0	2	0	0
Zollers, ss	0	0	4	5	2
Slack, 1b	0	0	14	1	1
Verga, 3b	0	0	0	2	0
Cross, 2b	0	0	3	0	0
MacMannis, lf	0	0	1	1	0
Brown, p	0	0	0	7	0
Robinson, rf	0	0	1	1	0
Totals	0	0	27	18	3

PHILADELPHIA GIANTS

	R.	H.	O.	A.	E.
Grant, 2b	0	1	1	2	0
Johnson, ss	0	0	0	0	0
Hill, lf	1	1	2	0	0
Monroe, ss	1	0	2	3	0
Moore, cf	1	1	2	0	0
Foster, p	0	0	2	5	0
Bowman, rf	0	1	1	1	0
Washington, c	0	0	5	0	0
Thomas, 1 b	0	0	12	1	1
Totals	3	4	27	12	0

Camden	0	0	0	0	0	0	0	0	0 – 0
Giants	0	1	0	2	0	0	0	0	0 – 3

Two base hits–Hill Bowman. Sacrifice hits–Brown, Foster. Left on bases–Camden, 3; Philadelphia Giants, 3. Struck out–By Brown, 2; by Foster, 5. Bases on balls–By Brown, 1; by Foster, 2. Time–1.30. Umpire–Osborn.

PHILA. GIANTS VS. CUBAN X-GIANTS
Atlantic City, Sept. 1, 1904

CAMDEN.

	R.	H.	O.	A.	E.
Meehan, cf	0	0	2	0	0
Miller, c	0	0	2	0	0
Zollers, ss	0	0	4	5	2
Slack, 1b	0	0	14	1	1
Verga, 3b	0	0	0	2	0
Cross, 2b	0	0	3	0	0
MacMannis, lf	0	0	1	1	0
Brown, p	0	0	0	7	0
Robinson, rf	0	0	1	1	0
Totals	0	0	27	18	3

PHILADELPHIA GIANTS.

	R.	H.	O.	A.	E.
Grant, 2b	0	1	1	2	0
Johnson, ss	0	0	0	0	0
Hill, lf	1	1	2	0	0
Monroe, ss	1	0	2	3	0
Moore, cf	1	1	2	0	0
Foster, p	0	0	2	5	0
Bowen, rf	0	1	1	1	0
Washington, c	0	0	5	0	0
Thomas, 1b	0	0	12	1	0
Totals	3	4	27	12	0

Camden ...... 0 0 0 0 0 0 0 0 0—0
Giants 0 1 0 2 0 0 0 0 0–3

Two base hits—Hill, Bowman. Sacrifice hits—Brown, Foster. Left on bases —Camden, 3; Philadelphia Giants, 3. Struck out—By Brown, 2; by Foster, 5. Bases on balls—By Brown, 1; by Foster, 2. Time—1.30. Umpire—Osborn.

PHILA. GIANTS VS. CUBAN X-GIANTS.

Atlantic City, Sept. 1, 1904.

PHILADELPHIA GIANTS.

	R.	H.	O.	A.	E.
Grant, 2b	1	1	0	1	0
Monroe, ss	1	0	1	1	1
White, 1b	0	0	5	0	0
Payne, lf	2	3	1	1	0

Boxscore of Rube Foster's no-hitter against Camden, reproduced from the original edition of White's Guide.

Philadelphia Giants, champions, season, 1905.

PHILADELPHIA GIANTS

	R.	H.	O.	A.	E.
Grant, 2b	1	1	0	1	1
Monroe, ss	1	0	1	1	1
White, 1b	0	0	5	0	0
Payne, lf	2	3	1	1	0
P. Hill, cf	1	1	1	0	0
Johnson, c	1	1	19	0	0
Foster, p	1	3	0	0	0
J. Hill, 3b	0	1	0	1	0
Footes, rf	1	0	0	1	0
Totals	8	10	27	5	1

CUBAN X-GIANTS

	R.	H.	O.	A.	E.
Johnson, ss	0	0	3	3	0
Patterson, 2b	2	2	4	2	0
Jordan, 1b	1	1	8	0	2
Moore, cf	0	1	1	0	3
Jackson, lf	0	1	1	0	0
Buckner, 1b	1	1	5	1	0

PHILA. GIANTS VS. CUBAN X-GIANTS.

Atlantic City, Sept. 3d, 1904.

PHILA. GIANTS.

	R.	H.	O.	A.	E.
Grant, 2b	1	1	1	3	0
White, 1b	1	2	11	1	2
Monroe, ss	0	0	2	2	0
Payne, lf	0	0	0	0	0
P. Hill, cf	0	0	0	0	0
Johnson, c	0	1	7	1	0
Foster, p	1	1	1	2	0
J. Hill, 3b	0	1	2	3	1
Bell, rf	1	0	3	0	0
Totals	4	6	27	12	3

CUBAN X-GIANTS.

	R.	H.	O.	A.	E.
Johnson, ss	1	1	3	0	1
Patterson, 2b	1	1	3	2	0
Jordan, 1b	0	0	9	1	0
Moore, cf	0	0	3	0	2
Buckner, rf	0	0	1	0	0
Jackson, lf	0	0	1	0	0
J. Smith, 3b	0	0	1	3	0
Williams, c	0	0	6	1	0
McClellan, p	0	0	0	2	0
Totals	2	2	27	9	3

Batteries—Foster and Johnson; McClellan and Williams. Struck out—By Foster, 5; by McClellan, 5. Umpires—Adams and Meher.

65

Boxscore of Philadelphia Giants–Cuban X-Giants game of 3 September 1904, reproduced from the original edition of White's Guide.

Smith, 3b	0	0	1	1	0
Williams, c	0	0	4	3	0
McClellan, p	0	0	0	2	0
Ball, p	4	7	27	12	5 [sic]
Totals	4	7	27	12	5

Batteries–Foster and Johnson; Ball and McClellan and Williams.
Struck out by Foster, 18; by Ball, 2; by McClellan, 2. Umpires, Adams
and Agnew.

PHILA. GIANTS VS. CUBAN X-GIANTS
Atlantic City, Sept. 3d, 1904

PHILADELPHIA GIANTS

	R.	H.	O.	A.	E.
Grant, 2b	1	1	1	7	0
White, 1b	1	2	11	1	3
Monroe, ss	0	0	2	2	0
Payne, lf	0	0	0	0	0
P. Hill, cf	0	0	0	0	0
Johnson, c	0	1	7	1	0
Foster, p	1	1	1	3	0
J. Hill, 3b	0	1	2	3	1
Bell, rf	1	0	3	0	0
Totals	4	6	27	17	3

CUBAN X-GIANTS

	R.	H.	O.	A.	E.
Johnson, ss	1	1	3	0	1
Patterson, 2b	1	1	3	2	0
Jordan, 1b	0	0	9	1	0
Moore, cf	0	0	2	0	2
Buckner, rf	0	0	1	0	0
Jackson, lf	0	0	1	0	0
J. Smith, 3b	0	0	1	3	0
Williams, c	0	0	6	1	0
McClellan, p	0	0	0	2	0
Totals	2	2	27	9	3

Batteries–Foster and Johnson: McClellan and Williams. Struck
out–By Foster, 5: by McClellan, 3. Umpires–Adams and Meber.

Horn, pitching for the Philadelphia Giants, shut the Oxford, Pa.,
team out without a hit or run in 1904.

H. Walter Schlichter "Slick," sporting editor, "Philadelphia Item," president, The National Association of Colored Baseball Clubs of the United States and Cuba. President and manager of the Philadelphia Giants B.B. and A.A., Inc.

Hopkins, of the Chicago Unions, has frequently struck out twelve and fifteen men in games with strong amateur and semi-professional teams of Chicago.

George Wilson, of Columbia Giants fame, has pitched some wonderful games against the strongest teams of the West. Wilson is one

Chas. "Kid" Carter, pitcher, Philadelphia Giants, 1902 to 1905.

of the most difficult men to hit among the colored pitchers. He is a bronzed "Waddell" when right.

Other pitchers that have done remarkable work and are considered to be present day stars, are: Billy Holland, of the Royal Giants; H. E. Buckner; John Davis, Leland Giants; Gatewood, Cuban X-Giants; Carter and Merritt of the Royal Giants; Sampson and Best of Genuine Cuban Giants; Washington, of Jacksonville, Fla.; Bowman, Philadelphia Giants; Foster, Philadelphia Giants, and others.

COLORED BASE BALL AS A PROFESSION

There is nothing like protecting the rights of the owners of base ball teams and while the ball players generally work in the opposite directions, they move under a false star and are only temporarily benefitted. The owner of a base ball team is in the business to make money for years to come, while the player is in the game to make the biggest rake off in the quickest time, never knowing just when he will have hard luck and fail to keep up a hot pace.

The colored ball player should always look before he leaps. He should remember that, although possessing the ability in every particular of the white ball player, he is not in a position to demand the same salary as his white brother, as the difference in the receipts of their respective games are decidedly in favor of the latter; thousands attending games of the whites to hundreds of the blacks. Leaving out the colored stars of the International League of 1887, the aggregate salaries for colored ball players, amounted to a little over $5,500 for a season of 5½ months. 1906, the banner year for colored base ball, when the number of teams is considered, with no less than 150 ball players employed in the professional ranks, they drew over $70,000 in salaries for the season, an average of $466 per man. An increase of over 785 per cent, from 1886 to 1907, or an average of 39¼ per cent increase each year.

These figures, in comparison, are expressly low to the salaries received and the business done by players and owners of white teams. Statistics of 1906 show the two major leagues alone paying

Andrew (Rube) Foster, pitcher, Philadelphia Giants, 1904 to 1907.

over $600,000 per season to more than 300 ball players. While the minor leagues pay over $2,000,000 to 3,500 players.

These figures give the major league players an average of $2,000 per man for a season's work; and the minor league players $571 per man. The disparity in the salary of a major league player and a colored player is enormous, especially when it is taken into consideration that, were it not for color, many would be playing in the big league for $2,000, or more per season instead of less than $500 per season. As it is, they receive less than the minor league player.

Base ball is a legitimate profession. As much so as any other vocation, and should be fostered by owners and players alike. It is indisputably a masculine game, demanding all manly qualities and powers to the extreme. It is immune from attacks from all critics. From a scientific standpoint it outclasses all other American games. It should be taken seriously by the colored player, as honest efforts with his great ability will open an avenue in the near future wherein he may walk hand-in-hand with the opposite race in the greatest of all American games – base ball.

MANAGERS TROUBLES

The tribulations of a manager of the base ball team, especially a colored team, are known only to those who have inside knowledge of the game and are familiar with what a base ball manager has to contend.

To deal with the question from an independent stand-point, it is found more difficult to handle a team in that respect than when a member of a league, under the National agreement. Rules laid down by league teams are easily enforced; from the fact that players in the minor organizations have aspirations to shine as stars in the major leagues and consequently cannot afford a reckless disregard of the rules to compel them to keep in condition for first-class ball playing. Once in the big league they have a horror of being relegated to the minors, which creates a greater respect for the rules.

In this day and time, when colored base ball teams are numerous and each striving for supremacy, the colored manager's path is not one of sunshine. With twelve or fourteen men under his command,

Charles Grant, second baseman, Philadelphia Giants.

twelve or fourteen different minds and dispositions to control and centre on the intricate points of play, with no National League of base ball clubs behind the rules and regulations, with the many complaints of players and threats of quitting ringing in his ears day after day, he passes many a sleepless night and will often ask for that "Patience he needs."

To guard against such contingencies, managers, should be careful in selecting players to compose a team. A player of mediocre

G. GRANT WILLIAMS

OUR ONLY COLORED DAILY PAPER

The Philadelphia Tribune

DAILY and WEEKLY

CHRIS. J. PERRY, *Publisher*.
G. GRANT WILLIAMS, *City Editor*.

Published every afternoon at
717 Sansom St., Philadelphia, Pa.

The best Medium for advertising when you want to reach the people.

G. *Grant Williams, city editor*, The Philadelphia Tribune.

J. P. Hill, left fielder, Philadelphia Giants.

ability who is a willing and hard worker and easily handled, is far better in every respect to a team than one of rare ability with so much self-importance as to create a feeling of antipathy among his fellow players.

It will be found that 80 per cent of these self-important players think so well of their individual reputations, that an error or misplay on their part during a game is liable to make them lose their nerve.

It is the man with the nerve that gets there, but in base ball there are two kinds of nerve. One kind is on the outside and the other on the inside. For a winner, the inside nerve is the best every time. A "four flusher" will make all kinds of noise with his mouth, but when it comes to a test on the ball field, will develop a "yellow streak" a yard long. The ball player with the nerve on the inside does but little talking about what he is going to do, but just watch the man when it comes to the game depending on quick action and he is invariably there.

Managers should possess gray matter and have up-to-date ideas. They should acquire a full understanding of the game and strive to instil it into the heads of his players. There is a general weakness among colored players that mitigates [sic] to a great extent against their success on the diamond, that is, their lack of knowledge and understanding of the playing rules. The rules should be thoroughly understood as games have been won and lost where the deciding play depended on the interpretation of a rule.

They should aim to blend the team into a highly polished and magnificent machine. The play itself is a science, if that term may be applied to sport. Compared to town ball or other old fashioned games, it suggests the present day harvesting engine and its prototype, the scythe.

The attitude of the spectators, or as they are popularly called "fans" has changed at about the same rate as the game. Formerly they were content with being amused and the game developed comedians like Abe Harrison and Bill Joyner. But now they demand faultless play. Genuine diversion is as scarce as the green carnation. Rugged, callous, fearless though he be, the player sel-

Dan McClellan, pitcher, Philadelphia Giants.

Emmett Bowman, pitcher, Philadelphia Giants.

dom volunteers any original fun-making on the field, or on the coaching-line, lest the "fans" take it amiss.

Not that the spectator is unwilling to be amused! He goes to the game with that hope and intention – so eager for amusement. Indeed, that if a player somersaults on a wet field, or another doffs his cap with a sly, unwonted grimace, after making a great catch. It provokes Heaven-splitting laughter.

On the other hand, mighty and bitter is the reward of wrath visited upon one who by lack of vigilance, activity or quickness brings disaster upon his team.

The funny man in colored base ball is becoming extinct. Where every man on a team would do a funny stunt during a game back in the eighties and early nineties, now will be found only one or two on a team who essays to amuse the spectators of the present day. Monroe, third baseman of the Royal Giants of Brooklyn is the leading fun-maker of the colored profession of to-day. His comic sayings and actions while on the field, together with his ability as a fielder, hitter and runner has earned for him a great reputation as a ball player. Joyner, of Chicago, draws a salary for fun-making alone. Pop Watkins, Gordon and Best of the Genuine Cuban Giants, are the other present day comedians of the diamond.

The majority of colored ball players are now carefully watching the scientific points of the game with a mind to perfect team work, base running, bunting, place hitting and every other department of the game is studied and discussed by the leading colored players which, if continued, will enable them, in the course of a few years, to cope successfully in every particular with the leading teams of the country.

THE COLOR LINE

In no other profession has the color line been drawn more rigidly than in base ball. As far back as 1872 the first colored ball player of note playing on a white team was Bud Fowler, the celebrated promoter of colored ball clubs, and the sage of base ball. But played on a New Castle, Pennsylvania, team that

Jas. Booker, catcher, Philadelphia Giants.

year. Later the Walker Brothers, Fleet and Weldy, played on prominent college teams of the West. Fleet Walker has the distinction of
being the only known colored player that ever played in one of the
big leagues. In 1884 Walker caught for Toledo in the old American
Association. At this time the Walker brothers and Bud Fowler were
the only negroes in the profession.

In 1886 Frank Grant joined Buffalo, of the International League.

In 1887 no less than twenty colored ball players scattered among
the different smaller leagues of the country.

With Walker, Grant, Stovy, Fowler, Higgins and Renfro in the
International League, White, W. Walker, N. Higgins and R. Johnson
in the Ohio League, and others in the West, made 1887 a banner
year for colored talent in the white leagues. But this year marked
the beginning of the elimination of colored players from white
clubs. All the leagues, during the Winter of 1887 and 1888, drew the
color line, or had a clause inserted in their constitutions limiting
the number of colored players to be employed by each club.

This color line has been agitated by A. C. Anson, Captain of the
Chicago National League team for years. As far back as 1883, Anson,
with his team, landed in Toledo, O., to play an exhibition game with
the American Association team. Walker, the colored catcher, was a
member of the Toledos at the time. Anson at first absolutely refused
to play his nine against Walker, the colored man, until he was told
he could either play with Walker on this team or take his nine off
the field. Anson in 1887 again refused to play the Newark Eastern
League with Stovey, the colored pitcher, in the box. Were it not for
this same man Anson, there would have been a colored player in
the National League in 1887. John W. Ward, of the New York club,
was anxious to secure Geo. Stovey and arrangements were about
completed for his transfer from the Newark club, when a brawl was
heard from Chicago to New York. The same Anson, with all the
venom of hate which would be worthy of a Tillman or a Vardaman
of the present day, made strenuous and fruitful opposition to any
proposition looking to the admittance of a colored man into the
National League. Just why Adrian C. Anson, manager and captain
of the Chicago National League Club, was so strongly opposed to
colored players on white teams cannot be explained. His repugnant

Philadelphia Giants, season, 1902.

feeling, shown at every opportunity, toward colored ball players, was a source of comment through every league in the country, and his opposition, with his great popularity and power in base ball circles, hastened the exclusion to the black man from the white leagues.

The colored players are not only barred from playing on white clubs, but at times games are canceled for no other reason than objections being raised by a Southern ball player, who refuses to play against a colored ball club. These men from the South who object to playing are, as a rule, fine ball players, and rather than lose their services, the managers will not book a colored team.

The colored ball player suffers great inconvenience, at times, while traveling. All hotels are generally filled from the cellar to the garret when they strike a town. It is a common occurrence for them to arrive in a city late at night and walk around for several hours before getting a place to lodge.

The situation is far different to-day in this respect than it was years ago. At one time the colored teams were accommodated in some of the best hotels in the country, as the entertainment in 1887 of the Cuban Giants at the McClure House in Wheeling, W. Va., will show.

The cause of this change is no doubt due to the condition of things from a racial standpoint. With the color question upper-most in the minds of the people at the present time, such proceedings on the part of hotel-keepers may be expected and will be difficult to remedy.

It is said on good authority that one of the leading players and a manager of the National League is advocating the entrance of colored players in the National League with a view of signing "Matthews," the colored man, late of Harvard. It is not expected that he will succeed in this advocacy of such a move, but when such actions come to notice there are grounds for hoping that some day the bar will drop and some good man will be chosen from out of the colored profession that will be a credit to all, and pave the way for others to follow.

This article would not be complete did we not mention the effort of John McGraw, manager of the New York National League, to sign a colored man for his Baltimore American League team.

While Manager McGraw was in Hot Springs, Ark., preparing to enter the season of 1901, he was attracted toward Chas. Grant, second baseman of the Columbia Giants of Chicago, who was also at Hot Springs, playing on a colored team. McGraw, whose knowledge of and capacity for base ball is surpassed by none, thought he saw in Grant a ball player and a card. With the color line so rigidly enforced in the American League, McGraw was at a loss as to how he could get Grant for his Baltimore bunch. The little Napoleon of base ball with a brain for solving intricate circumstances in base ball transactions, conceived the idea of introducing Grant in the league as an Indian. Had it not been for friends of Grant being so eager to show their esteem while the Baltimores were playing in Chicago, McGraw's little scheme would have worked nicely. As it was the bouquet tendered to Grant, which was meant as a gift for the colored man, was really his undoing. McGraw was immediately

Philadelphia Giants booking advertisement.

notified to release Grant at once, as colored players would not be
tolerated in the league. This shows what a base ball man will do to
get a winner and also shows why McGraw has been called by many,
the greatest of all base ball managers.

The following open letter was sent to President McDermit, of the
Tri-State (formerly Ohio) League, by Weldy Walker, a member of
the Akron, O., team of 1887, which speaks for itself.

The letter was dated March 5th, 1888. The law prohibiting the
employment of colored players in the league was rescinded a few
weeks later.

Steubenville, O., March 5 – Mr. McDermit, President Tri-State

Royal Giants, of Brooklyn, season, 1906.

League – Sir: I take the liberty of addressing you because noticing in The Sporting Life that the "law," permitting colored men to sign was repealed, etc., at the special meeting held at Columbus, February 22, of the above-named League of which you are the president. I ascertaining the reason of such an action I have grievances, it is a question with me whether individual loss subserves the public good in this case. This is the only question to be considered – both morally and financially – in this, as it is, or ought to be, in all cases that convinced beyond doubt that you all, as a body of men, have not been impartial and unprejudiced in your consideration of the great and important question – the success of the "National game."

The reason I say this is because you have shown partiality by making an exception with a member of the Zanesville Club, and from this one would infer that he is the only one of the three colored players – Dick Johnson, alias Dick Neale, alias Dick Noyle, as the Sporting Life correspondent from Columbus has it; Sol White, of the Wheelings, whom I must compliment by saying was one, if not the surest hitter in the Ohio League last year, and your humble servant, who was unfortunate enough to join the Akron just ten days before they busted.

It is not because I was reserved and have been denied making my bread and butter with some clubs that I speak; but it is in hopes that the action taken at your last meeting will be called up for reconsideration at your next.

The law is a disgrace to the present age, and reflect very much upon the intelligence of your last meeting, and casts derision at the laws of Ohio – the voice of the people – that says all men are equal. I would suggest that your honorable body, in case that black law is not repealed, pass one making it criminal for a colored man or woman to be found in a ball ground.

There is now the same accommodation made for the colored patron of the game as the white, and the same provision and dispensation is made for the money of them both that finds its way into the coffers of the various clubs.

There should be some broader cause – such as lack of ability, behavior and intelligence – for barring a player, rather than his color. It is for these reasons and because I think ability and intelligence should be recognized first and last – at all times and by everyone – I ask the question again why was the "law permitting colored men to sign repealed, etc.?"

Yours truly,

WELDY W. WALKER

OLD TIMERS COMPARED

The colored ball players of to-day are just as fast as those of years ago. They hit as well, field as well and are just as speedy on their feet as the boys of the late '80's and early '90's were when at their best. But are they as good as the old ones were when together as a team?

It is a well known fact that a base ball team composed of all star players never won a pennant. When you see a team of all star ball players, you will find individuality a very prominent feature in their style of play. Individuality is a great hindrance to team work and without team work a team stands a poor chance of beating a bunch of ball players that play the game.

There is a vast difference in the disposition of the ball player of

J. W. Connor, owner and manager, Royal Giants, of Brooklyn.

John W. Connor

Royal Cafe
AND
Palm Garden

"*John W. Connor Royal Cafe and Palm Garden*" *advertisement;* "*176 Myrtle Avenue, Brooklyn, New York. Headquarters, Royal Giants. Music and Entertainment every evening.*"

Grant (Home Run) Johnson, captain and shortstop, Royal Giants.

Wm. S. Munroe, third baseman, Royal Giants.

to-day than that of the old timers. They do not take to other athletic sports as the old boys used to do when afforded the opportunity. Swimming, rowing, boxing and sprinting contests were of frequent occurrence with the boys of the early '90's, while the players of to-day are satisfied to attend such contests as spectators only.

As a comparison of the merits of the old ball teams with the teams of late years, the team of 1891 called the Big Gorhams, was the best of the old bunch, and the Philadelphia Giants of 1905 the best of the colored ball players since 1891. This selection is not

Geo. (Chappy) Johnson, catcher, Royal Giants of Brooklyn.

Wm. Holland, pitcher, Royal Giants of Brooklyn.

Harry Buckner, pitcher, Royal Giants of Brooklyn.

meant to discredit the great playing of the Cuban Giants of 1894, the Chicago Unions of 1898 and '99, the Columbia Giants of 1899 and 1900, the Cuban X-Giants of 1901 to 1904, but individually and collectively in the opinion of the majority of fans that have followed colored base ball from its infancy the Gorhams of 1891 and the Philadelphia Giants of 1905 were the premier of their respective times. The line-up of both teams were:

Gorhams of 1891		Phila. Giants of 1905
Clarence Williams	Catcher	James Booker
Arthur Thomas	Catcher	Tom Washington
Geo. Stovey	Pitcher	Dan McClellan
Wm. Selden	Pitcher	Andrew Foster
Wm. Malone	Pitcher	Emmett Bowman
Geo. Williams	First Base	Sol White
Sol White	Second Base	Chas. Grant
Andrew Jackson	Third Base	Wm. Monroe
Frank Grant	Short Stop	Grant Johnson
Malone or Selden	Left Field	J. Preston Hill
Oscar Jackson	Centre Field	Harry Moore
Thomas or Williams	Right Field	Bowman, McClellan or Foster

A series of games between these two teams would have been worth going miles to see and would have rivaled the late world's series which was played in Chicago.

THE CUBANS

The Cuban teams have shown a wonderful improvement in their style of play since their first visit to this country, which is no doubt due to the observation of the style and system by which the American ball teams play the game. The Cuban players gave everything that constitute good ball playing with the exception of inside work. They are wonderful fielders, strong throwers and fast runners. They lack the baseball nerve or staying qualities, which shows so prominently in the American play-

Robert Footes, catcher, Royal Giants of Brooklyn.

"La Flor de Manuel Camps" Cuban tobacco advertisement.

ers and many games are deliberately thrown away by the Cubans when they think the umpire has made a mistake or when one of their number is guilty of a misplay.

Bunting was an unknown art with the Cuban player until the past two or three seasons. Now, they seem to be particularly in love with the squeeze play, and they are always pleased when the occasion offers the opportunity to pull it off.

The Cubans are great for all around work. They all seem able to play any position on the diamond and play it well.

Of the many Cuban teams that have visited America, the stronger was the Cuban Stars of Santiago de Cuba. They were organized in 1905 and composed of all Cuban players. Their American manager is Manuel Camps, of Brooklyn, N.Y. This team is the only Cuban team in the National Association of Colored Base Ball Clubs of the United States and Cuba.

The leading Cuban player in the estimation of the American public is Bustamante, short-stop of the Cuban Stars, although this player is not as fast as he was three seasons back. While he is still considered one of the best in the profession he does not show the form at the bat nor on bases as when he first made his appearance

MANUEL CAMPS
Owner and Manager
Cuban Stars

Manuel Camps, owner and manager, Cuban Stars.

in America. Being a natural player his lack of form is no doubt, due to staleness.

Cuban players are in the game Winter and Summer, and of a necessity become stale in the course of a short time.

Players like Almeida, Palimino, Garcia, Valdes, Molina, Prats

Luis Bustamante, shortstop, Cuban Stars.

Pedro Medina, catcher, Cuban Stars.

George (Chappie) Johnson, first baseman, Columbia Giants, 1899–1900.

Perez and other stars of Cuba should take a season's rest. It would add several years to their base ball career.

HOW TO PITCH

by Andrew Foster

I t has been clearly demonstrated in the history of the national game of base ball that all positions need men that can play their respective positions and play them well. But it matters not how strong the infield or outfield may be, or how fast a team is on the bases, the main strength of all base ball nines lies in their pitchers. It does seem strange that a team composed of star players of to-day are weak without some first-class pitchers. It is common occurrence to hear or read the report of a game of ball where the headlines read, "He pitched great ball, but his support was bad," or "they never hit behind him," or "he was wild and in-effective." Sometimes the pitchers get great credit, especially when he has had support. There is always sympathy expressed for him, showing plainly the responsibility resting on his shoulders.

Any pitcher who expects to pitch regularly or play professional ball should first learn the essentials of making a pitcher.

Some people consider a young pitcher with terrific speed and a variety of curves a wonder, but the experienced base ball "fan" will watch his work for some time before they class him with the star twirlers. I have seen young pitchers at times pitch wonderful ball when receiving extraordinary support, but they never stop to think that it matters not how much speed or how fast their balls break, or how they fool the batter, that the batter is daily figuring on him and it is only a matter of time before they will solve his delivery. Being used to fooling batters, some pitchers, when they get hit, become worried and they will say "they don't break right for me to-day." Everything may work wrong for awhile and people will begin to lose confidence in him, especially if he is a youngster in fast company.

So many pitchers ruin their chances by not being in condition. Condition is the main essential to pitching. Some pitchers are better

John W. Patterson, manager, Columbia Giants of Chicago, 1899–1900.

Wm. Brown, Asst. manager, Leland Giants of Chicago, 1906.

in warm weather than in cold weather. A pitcher should never fully let out until his arm becomes warm and limbered up. I have lost games by not being warmed up; but what is a game, to a pitcher's arm?

This is particularly true with the young pitcher who may be called in to replace a pitcher who is being hit. Naturally every pitcher has pride, and very few object to being made a hero of. It is natural that he should want to save the game, and so is likely to forget to get into the pitching gradually and is more than likely to thus permanently injure his arm.

I have a theory of pitching that has helped me considerably. A pitcher should have control of every ball he pitches. But it matters not how good a pitcher is, he will become wild at times and can't get them over. Do not become disheartened at that, don't slacken your speed to get a ball over the plate, but teach yourself to master the weakness. Some pitchers when they have three balls and two strikes on the batter, often bring the ball straight over the plate and as the batter is always looking for it that way he will possibly "break up the game" for you. I use a curve ball mostly when in the hole. In the first place, the batter is not looking for it, and secondly they will hit at a curve quicker as it may come over the plate, and if not, they are liable to be fooled. Most pitchers in the independent teams use a fast ball close to the batter which the batter can easily see will be on the in-corner of the plate and they get their eye on it very easy.

A pitcher should learn to field his position. Always try to get a ball in a position to throw it.

The real test comes when you are pitching with men on bases. Do not worry. Try to appear jolly and unconcerned. I have smiled often with the bases full with two strikes and three balls on the batter. This seems to unnerve them. In other instances, where the batter appears anxious to hit waste a little time on him, and when you think he realizes his position and everybody yelling for him to hit it out, waste a few balls and try his nerve; the majority of times you will win out by drawing him into hitting at a wide one.

I often sit on the bench and watch the opposing teams' batting practice to see how they swing at a ball and I gain a great deal by it. Try everything you can on a batter, and if he hits, don't become discouraged. Batters often have a day on and will hit any kind of ball, no matter where you put it.

The three great principles of pitching are good control, when to pitch certain balls, and where to pitch them. The longer you are in the game, the more you should gain by experience. Where inexperience will lose many games, nerve and experience will bring you out victor.

If at first you don't succeed, try again.

ANDREW FOSTER

ART AND SCIENCE OF HITTING

by Grant (Home Run) Johnson

There are a number of requisites that a player should possess to be a first-class hitter, but in my opinion, two of the greatest and most essential ones are confidence and fearlessness. If, because of the reputation of the pitcher opposing you, your confidence in your ability to hit him is lacking, or you fear being hit by his wonderful speed or have the least fear in your heart at all, your success at such a time is indeed doubtful. If you possess both of these essentials, then it is an easy matter for the earnest student of hitting to acquire the science and judgment. Most young players make the natural mistake of trying to become home-run hitters and hit the ball with all the force at their command at all times with a full swing of the bat. This is a serious mistake and a great detriment to good batting.

In swinging the bat with all your might, you in a measure, lose sight of the ball and also change the course you intended the bat to go, and even if only the fraction of an inch, it will not meet the ball fairly, which results as a rule, in a comparatively easy chance for the opposing fielders. At a critical period of a game the experienced pitcher would far prefer pitching to the mighty swinger to the cool steady batter who tries to meet the ball and place it to the best advantage. My advice to young players is secure a bat which you can handle perfectly, catch well upon it and in taking your position at the plate, be sure and stand firmly and face the pitcher, thinking

Bert Williams, of Williams and Walker, manager and first baseman,
W. & W.B.B.C., and all around "fan."

you are going to hit without the least atom of fear about you. Seldom strike at the first ball pitched, as in letting it pass you get a line on the speed or curve of the pitcher. As he delivers one to your liking, try to meet it fairly, and when successful you will be surprised, and gratified, at the distance of the hit, with only ordinary force behind the swing. To improve the eye, I find bunting to be very effective, and should be practiced before each game as a player who can both hit and bunt is a very valuable man to any team.

GRANT JOHNSON

CASEY AT THE BAT

The outlook wasn't brilliant for the Mudville nine that day;
The score stood four to two with but one inning more to play,
And then when Cooney died at first and Barrows did the same,
A sickly silence fell upon the patrons of the game.

A straggling few got up to go in deep despair. The rest
clung to that hope which springs eternal in the human breast;
They thought if only Casey could get a whack at that –
We'd put up even money yet with Casey at the bat.

But Flynn preceded Casey, as did also Jimmie Blake,
And the former was a Lula, and latter was a cake,
So upon that stricken multitude grim melancholy sat,
For there seemed but little chance of Casey coming to the bat.

But Flynn let drive a single to the wonderment of all,
And Blake, the much despised, tore the cover off the ball;
And when the smoke was lifted, and the men saw what had
    occurred,
There was Johnnie safe at second and Flynn a-hugging third.

Then from five thousand throats or more there rose a lusty yell;
It rumbled through the valley, it rattled through the dell;
It knocked upon the mountain and recoiled upon the flat,
For Casey, mighty Casey, was advanc[ing] to the bat.

There was ease in Casey's manner as he stepped into his place;
There was pride in Casey's bearing and a smile on Casey's face.

Frank Grant, second baseman, for Buffalo, International League Team, 1888.
The greatest base ball player of his age.

W. W. Walker, catcher, Akron, O. League team, 1887.

And when, responding to the cheers, he lightly doffed his hat,
No stranger in the crowd could doubt 'twas Casey at the bat.

Ten thousand eyes were on him as he rubbed his hands with dirt,
Five thousand tongues applauded as he wiped them on his shirt,
Then while the writhing pitcher ground the ball into his hip,
Defiance gleamed in Casey's eye, a sneer curled Casey's lip.

And now the leather-covered sphere came hurtling through the
   air,
And Casey stood a watching it in hauty grandeur there,
Close by the sturdy batsman the ball unheeded sped –
"That ain't my style," said Casey.
"Strike one," the umpire said.

From the benches black with people, there went up a muffled roar,
Like the beating of the storm waves on a stern and distant shore.
Kill him! Kill the umpire! shouted some one on the stand;
And its likely they'd have killed him had not Casey raised his
   hand.

With a smile of Christian charity great Casey's visage shone.
He stilled the rising tumult; he bade the game go on;
He signaled to the pitcher and once more the spheroid flew;
But Casey still ignored it and the umpire said, "Strike two!"

"Fraud!" cried the maddened thousands, and the echo answered
   fraud,
But one scornful look from Casey and the multitude was awed.
They saw his face grow stern and cold, they saw his muscles strain,
And they knew that Casey wouldn't let that ball go by again.

The sneer has gone from Casey's lip, his teeth are clinched in hate;
He pounds with cruel violence his bat upon the plate.
And now the pitcher holds the ball and now he lets it go,
And now the air is shattered by the force of Casey's blow.

Oh! somewhere in this favored land the sun is shining bright;
The band is playing somewhere and somewhere hearts are light,

*Championship Cup, International League, won by Philadelphia Giants,
season, 1906.*

*The Royal Poinciana Base Ball Team of Palm Beach, Fla., season, 1906.
A combination hard to beat.*

And somewhere men are laughing, and somewhere children
   shout,
But there is no joy in Mudville – mighty Casey has struck out.

WHEN CASEY SLUGGED THE BALL

Oh, you all have heard of Mudville.
   Heard of mighty Casey, too;
Of the groans amid the bleachers
   As the ball thrice past him flew;
But you haven't heard the story,
   The best story of them all,
Of the day in happy Mudville,
   When great Casey slugged the ball.

'Twas the day they played "the Giants,"
  And the score stood ten to eight;
Two men were on the bases,
  And great Casey at the plate.
"Swipe her, Casey," yelled the rooters,
  And the hero doffed his cap;
Three to win and two to tie,
  And Casey at the bat.

Mid a hush of expectation,
  Now the ball flies past his head;
Great Casey grins a sickly grin;
  "Strike one," the umpire said.
Again the pitcher raised his arm,
  Again the horse-hide flew;
Great Casey spat upon the ground,
  And the umpire said, "Strike two."

"It's a roast," came from the grandstand,
  "He is bought without a doubt!"
"He is rotten!" roared the bleachers,
  "Throw the daylight robber out!"
"I'll break yer face," says Casey,
  "That one went below my knee;
"If I miss the next, ye blackguard
  "Ye won't live long to see."

The next one came like lightning,
  And the umpire held his breath,
For well he knew if Casey missed,
  'Twould surely mean his death!
But Casey swung to meet it,
  Backed by all his nerve and gall; –
Oh, if you had but heard the yell,
  As Casey smashed the ball!

He caught the pigskin on the nose,
  It cleared the big town lot,

Nat C. Strong, secretary, National Association Colored Base Ball Clubs of the United States and Cuba.

It sailed above the high church tower,
In vain the fielders sought;
And Casey didn't even run,
He stopped awhile to talk,
And then amid the deafening cheers
He came round in a walk.

And now he keeps a beer saloon;
He is Mayor of the town.
The people flock to see him
From all the country round;
And you need not look for Mudville
On the map upon the wall,
Because the town is called Caseyville,
Since Casey slugged the ball.

NAT WRIGHT

COLORED PLAYERS AND THE LEAGUE

It was clearly demonstrated that colored players pos-
sessed major league qualifications when such players
as Fleet Walker, Geo. Stovey, Frank Grant and Bud Fowler as members of the International League, back in the eighties, were stars of
a class "A" organization. All of these men would have been drafted
by the National League or the American Association had they been
of the opposite complexion. When Stovy and Walker were paired as
a battery, they were considered the stars of the country. Grant and
Fowler, as infielders, had no equals in the International League.

Frank Grant, in those days, was the base ball marvel. His playing
was a revelation to his fellow team mates, as well as the spectators.
In hitting he ranked with the best and his fielding bordered on the
impossible. Grant was a born ball player. He started as a catcher
when very young and it is said that during a game in Plattsburg,
N.Y., while catching, he ran to a telegraph pole and climbing up
about eight feet caught a foul fly. Otherwise it would have gone out
of his reach over an embankment. Grant was always quiet and

World's Champions: Philadelphia Giants, season, 1906.

unassuming on the ball field, never protesting a decision of an umpire, nor resenting an action of an opposing player. He was the greatest card in the profession.

George Williams, captain of the original Cuban Giants, was a great player and would have been one of the chosen number for a big league berth. Billy Whyte, Arthur Thomas, Clarence Williams, Ben Boyd and Ben Holmes, the crack third-baseman, would have been slated for the National League and made good.

Selden, of the Cuban Giants, of 1887, was one of the leading colored pitchers as late as 1899.

Of the players of to-day, with the same prospects for a future as the white players there would be a score or more colored ball players cavorting around the National League or American League diamonds at the present time.

As it is, the field for the colored professional is limited to a very

William Reynolds

Saloon

12th and Bainbridge Streets

PHILADELPHIA

Bell Phone Filbert 5999 D

William Reynolds Saloon advertisement.

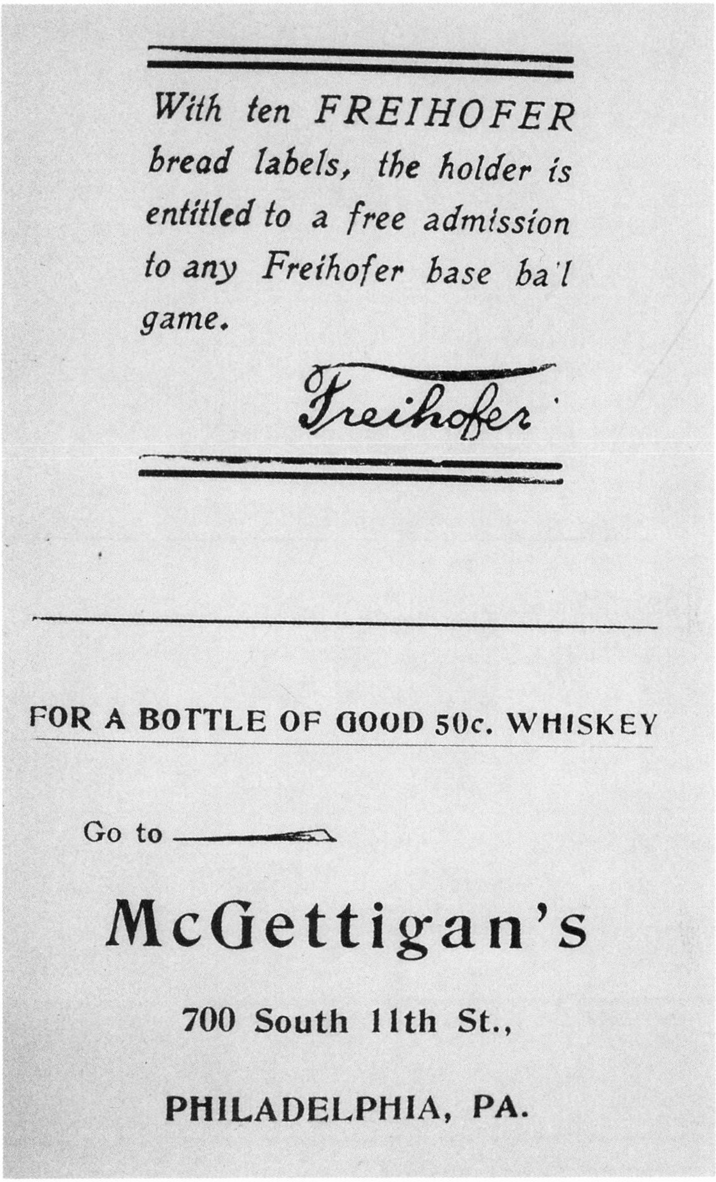

With ten *FREIHOFER* bread labels, the holder is entitled to a free admission to any Freihofer base ba'l game.

Freihofer

FOR A BOTTLE OF GOOD 50c. WHISKEY

Go to ————

McGettigan's

700 South 11th St.,

PHILADELPHIA, PA.

Freihofer Bread/McGettigan's Saloon ("Golden Age whiskey a specialty") advertisements.

Saloon

1311 Poplar St.,

PHILADELPHIA, PA.

A. A. COLEMAN

ONE OF THE "FANS

George Stæhle Saloon/A. A. Coleman advertisements.

J. W. JOHNSON

Pool Parlors
CIGARS & TOBACCO

1306 Poplar Street,
PHILADELPHIA, - - - PENNA.

BISHOP ROBINSON'S

SHAVING & HAIR CUTTING
EMPORIUM

1234 Melon St., Philadelphia, Pa

Special Line of all kinds of Perfumery, Hair Tonic, etc. for sale at moderate prices. Razors put in order a specialty.

John J. Rouse

SALOON

Business card advertisements (Rouse Saloon card went on to read "700 North 13th Street, Philadelphia, Penna.").

Raymond Wilson

Cigars and Tobacco

1539½ RIDGE AVE.

BELL PHONE   PHILA., PA.

Chauffeurs Rest

691 North 13th St.
OAKLEY & MARTIN, Prop.

High Grade Cigars and Tobacco
First class pool parlors

☞ *Headquarters of North Philadelphia Sports*

CHOICE WINES & LIQUORS

James Bigley

*Business card advertisements (Bigley ad went on to read
"Fine Cigars / 13th and Ogden Streets, Phila. PA").*

Hotel Scott advertisement.

narrow scope in the base ball world. When he looks into the future he sees no place for him on the Chicago Americans or Nationals (champions), nor the Athletics (American), or New York (National, ex-champions), even were he superior to Lajoie, or Wagner, Waddell or Mathewson, Kling or Schrock. Consequently, he loses interest. He knows that, so far shall I go, and no farther, and, as it is with the profession, so it is with his ability.

In naming a few of the many colored players of Major League calibre, we are not unmindful of those who are yet to come and are held back because of the small number of colored teams.

Of the catchers at present, the veteran, Clarence Williams, is very good, owing to his many years of base ball he would be taken as a good man for young pitchers: George (Chappie) Johnson, Bob Footes; Robinson, of Leland Giants, Petway, of Philadelphia Giants.

There are many colored pitchers who would no doubt land in the big league. McClellan, Bowman, Foster, Holland, Merritt, George Washington (Georgia Rabbit) Ball, Wilson, Davis and Buckner; the colored profession has great all-round players in Monroe, Bowman, Wright, Smith, Moore, G. Johnson, Talbert, P. Hill, C. Grant, Harris, Nelson, Francis, Patterson, Earl and many others.

2 HISTORY OF COLORED BASE-BALL DURING 1907
Sol White

After twenty-two years of professional life colored base ball has taken a firm hold on the hearts of the sport-loving public, and in every section of the United States one or more professional teams are being organized and efforts put forth to form a National League of Colored Base Ball Clubs.

From the beginning of colored base ball there has been an over-crowded market of base ball talent, and the demand has never been so great but that the supply was greater. The limited field for colored players has kept many first-class artists in the background, and the present time finds managers besieged with applications by ball players from all over the country, notwithstanding the great increase in the number of professional teams. The records made in 1907 by the rejuvenated Leland Giants, of Chicago, and the newly organized professional team of St. Paul, Minn., has thrown the West in a fever of enthusiasm that bids fair to culminate in the formation of a National League of Colored Base Ball Teams, which will greatly augment the chances for employment of colored talent so eager to obtain an opportunity to display their ability as exponents of the national game.

The leading teams of the West in the year of 1907 were Leland Giants and Chicago Unions, of Chicago; the St. Paul team, of St. Paul, Minn.; Indianapolis, Ind., and Louisville, Ky. This number will be increased in 1908 by teams in the following cities: Cleveland, Cincinnati, St. Louis and Pittsburg.

Philadelphia, the home of the colored champions, Philadelphia Giants, was further represented on the diamond by the Anchor Giants, managed by Henry Sellars; the Keystone Giants, under the management of Mr. Human, and the Defiance team, which was looked after by Lefty Myers, the veteran catcher. The "Quaker Giants," promoted by a stock company of well-known colored business men, with A. A. Coleman as manager-in-chief, and Harry Daniels, secretary, will be a new acquisition to Philadelphia's popular base ball teams of 1908. In addition to the Royal Giants, Cuban Giants and the New York Giants, Greater New York will have a new team, under the management of John (Pop) Watkins, ex-captain of the Cuban Giants, and a popular catcher. This will give the United States not less than eighteen professional colored base ball teams, with good, substantial backing, with prospects of several more before the end of 1908. If interest continues as great in the next few years as it has since 1904, we can look for colored leagues along the same lines of the American and National League organizations, which will give employment and protection to the vast number of players who are now asking for recognition. It is a good business proposition and should be looked into at once by the progressive promoters of base ball.

The season of 1907 lacked the enthusiasm displayed during the season of 1906 in the East, but never-the-less a review of the championship games between the teams representing the International League of Colored Base Ball Teams will be quite interesting as all the games were bitterly contested and desperately fought to the end.

An agreement between the Philadelphia Giants, of Phila., the Cuban Giants, of New York, the Royal Giants of Brooklyn and the Cuban Stars, of Havana, Cuba, called for five games between each team.

The team winning the greater number of games to be declared colored champions.

By winning a series from each team the Phila. Giants, for the fourth successive season won the colored championship. The Cuban Giants won second place, the Royal Giants third, and the Cuban Stars fourth.

The following are some of the most interesting contests:

At Brooklyn –

BROOKLYN ROYAL GIANTS

	R.	H.	O.	A.	E.
Johnson, shortstop	1	2	4	2	3
James, second base	0	0	2	5	1
Buckner, centre field	0	2	0	0	0
Milliner, right field	0	0	0	0	0
Holland, pitcher	0	0	0	3	0
Jordan, first base	0	0	15	1	0
J. Hill, third base	0	2	0	2	2
G. Johnson, catcher	0	0	3	2	0
Merritt, left field	0	0	0	0	0
Totals	1	6	24	15	6

PHILADELPHIA GIANTS

	R.	H.	O.	A.	E.
Grant, second base	1	0	0	2	0
P. Hill, left field	0	0	3	0	0
McClellan, pitcher	0	1	1	1	0
Binga, right field	0	1	3	0	0
Lloyd, shortstop	1	1	2	8	0
Bowman, centre field	0	0	1	0	0
Petway, catcher	1	0	2	0	0
R. Wilson, first base	1	1	15	0	0
Francis, third base.	1	0	0	3	0
Totals	5	4	27	14	0

Score by innings.

Phila. Giants	0	0	1	0	0	0	4	0	x - 5
B. Royal G.	0	0	0	0	0	0	0	0	1 - 1

Left on bases—Royals, 4; Phillies 3. Two base hits—Buckner, McClellan. Three base hits—Grant, Johnson. Home run—Lloyd. Stolen bases—R. Wilson, Francis. Double plays—Lloyd, Grant and Wilson, Milliner, Holland and Jordan. Struck out by—Holland, 2; McClellan, 3. Passed balls Johnson. Umpire—Dick Hassett. Attendance—3,000.

ROYAL GIANTS.

	R.	H.	O.	A.	E.
Monroe, third base	2	1	4	3	o
Bustamante, second base	o	1	1	3	o
Patterson, left field	o	1	o	o	o
Johnson, short stop	1	1	3	9	o
Buckner, pitcher	o	o	o	o	o
Milliner, right field	o	1	o	o	o
Bradley, catcher	1	1	5	o	o
Jordan, first base	o	1	11	o	o
Merritt, centre field	2	2	3	2	o
Totals	6	9	27	17	o

PHILADELPHIA GIANTS

	R.	H.	O.	A.	E.
Grant, second base	o	o	4	o	o
Hill, left field	o	1	2	o	o
McClellan, centre field	1	1	1	o	o
Lloyd, short stop	2	2	3	4	o
Petway, catcher	1	2	4	1	o
Mongin, third base	1	2	1	2	2
R. Wilson, first base	o	o	10	o	o
E. Wilson, pitcher	o	o	o	2	o
White, right field	o	o	2	o	o
Griffin, pitcher	o	o	o	1	1
Totals	5	8	27	10	3

Royal Giants	o	o	2	1	1	o	2	o	o – 6
Phila. Giants	o	o	o	o	o	o	3	o	2 – 5

Two-base hits–Hill, McClellan, Petway, Patterson, Lloyd. Two-base hit–Mongin. Home run–Mongin. Double plays–Lloyd to Wilson; Grant to Wilson. Stolen bases–Merritt, Munroe, Bushamonte. Struck out–By Buckner, 3; by Wilson, 1. First base on called balls–Off Wilson, 1; off Griffith, 1; off Buckner, 2. Time–1.45. Umpires–Mehrer and Shaner.

At Elizabethport:

	R.	H.	O.	A.	E.
Johnson, ss	1	1	3	2	3
Patterson, lf	0	0	2	0	1
Hill, 3b	0	0	1	3	1
Buckner, cf. p	0	1	1	3	0
James, 3b	0	0	1	1	0
Milliner, rf	0	1	2	0	0
Jordan, 1b	0	3	7	2	0
G. Johnson, c	0	2	4	4	1
Merritt, p	0	0	0	0	0
Holland, cf	0	0	3	0	1
*Williams	0	1	0	0	0
Totals	1	9	24	15	7

*Batted for Johnson in the ninth.

PHILA. GIANTS

	R.	H.	O.	A.	E.
Grant, 2b	1	1	1	1	2
Hill, lf	2	3	2	0	0
McClellan, cf	1	1	2	1	0
Binga, rf	1	1	1	0	0
Lloyd, ss	0	0	5	3	1
Bowman, p	1	2	1	3	1
Petway, c	1	3	6	1	2
Wilson, 1b	0	2	8	1	1
Francis, 3b	0	1	1	1	0
Totals	1	9	24	15	7

Royal Giants	0	0	1	0	0	0	0	0	0 - 1
Phila. Giants	4	0	0	0	0	0	3	0	x - 7

First base on balls-Off Bowman, 2; off Buckner, 5. Two base hits-Binga, Petway, G. Johnson. Three base hit-Buckner. Home runs-Grant, Hill. Sacrifice hit-Holland. Struck out-By Bowman, 5; Merritt, 1; Buckner, 2. Left on bases-Royal Giants, 4; Philadelphia Giants, 1. Wild pitch–Bowman. Stolen bases–Hill, Francis, Milliner. Time–1.35. Umpire–Bradley. Attendance, 2,000.

At Atlantic City –

	R.	H.	O.	A.	E.
Bus'te, ss	1	1	1	3	1
Carvallo, 1b	1	2	6	1	0
Almeida, 3b	1	0	3	2	0
Prats, rf	1	2	3	1	0
Munoz, cf	2	0	2	1	0
Mag'nat, lf	0	1	2	1	0
Ramos, 2b	0	1	2	2	0
Fig'ralla, c	0	1	8	1	0
Medina, p	0	0	0	2	0
Totals	6	8	27	14	1

	R.	H.	O.	A.	E.
Grant, 2b	2	2	0	3	0
Hill, lf	1	1	0	1	0
McClellan, cf	1	2	2	0	0
Lloyd, ss	0	1	1	5	0
Bowman, p	1	2	0	3	0
Mongin, 3b	0	2	2	1	2
Williams, c	1	2	3	0	0
White, rf	0	0	7	1	0
Petway, rf	1	0	2	0	0
R. Wilson, 1b	0	1	16	1	0
Totals	7	13	27	15	2

Phila. Giants . . . . 1 0 1 0 0 0 2 3 0 – 7
Cuban Stars . . . . 3 0 0 0 1 0 0 2 0 – 6

Second game –

	R.	H.	O.	A.	E.
Grant, 2b	1	1	1	1	0
Hill, lf	1	2	3	0	0
McClellan, p	0	2	0	1	0
Lloyd, ss	0	0	3	3	0
Bowman, cf	0	1	1	0	0
Petway, c..................	1	1	4	1	0
Mongin, 3b	1	1	1	3	1
R. Wilson, 1b	1	1	7	0	0
E. Wilson, rf	1	0	1	0	0
Totals	6	9	21	9	1

ROYAL GIANTS

	R.	H.	O.	A.	E.
Monroe, 3b	0	0	1	0	0
Bust'te, 2b	1	1	0	2	0
Johnson, ss	0	1	1	4	0
Buckner, p	0	0	1	2	0
Bradley, c	0	0	5	1	0
Patterson, lf	0	1	0	0	0
James, rf..................	0	0	0	0	0
Jordon, 1b.................	0	0	8	0	0
Merritt, cf	0	0	2	0	0
Totals	1	3	18	9	0

Phila. Giants	0	5	0	0	1	0	x – 6
Royal Giants	1	0	0	0	0	0	0 – 1

At Hoboken: –

HOBOKEN

	R.	H.	O.	A.	E.
Gregan, 1b	0	0	15	0	0
Hoffman, lf	0	1	3	0	0
Maloney, cf	0	0	4	0	0

	R.	H.	O.	A.	E.
Geon, p	0	1	0	2	0
Bassford, rf	0	0	2	0	0
Cainfield, ss	0	1	1	4	1
Green, c	0	0	4	2	0
Mack, 2b	0	2	2	4	0
Thomas, 3b	0	0	4	6	0
Totals	0	5	36	18	1

PHILADELPHIA GIANTS

	R.	H.	O.	A.	E.
Grant, 2b	0	0	2	1	0
Hill, lf	1	1	1	2	0
McClellan, p	0	0	0	0	0
Lloyd, ss	0	1	2	2	0
Bowman, cf	0	2	1	0	0
Petway, rf	0	0	2	0	0
Mongin, 3b	0	0	1	4	0
Wilson, 1b	0	0	15	0	0
Williams, c.......................	0	2	12	1	0
Totals	1	8	36	13	0

Phila. Giants ... 0 0 0 0 0 0 0 0 0 0 1–7

Hoboken 0 0 0 0 0 0 0 0 0 0 0–0

Two base hit–Hill. Base on balls–Off McClellan, 1. Struck out–By McClellan, 9; by Geon, 2. Left on bases–Hoboken, 5; Phila. Giants, 4. Hit by pitcher–By McClellan, 2. Umpire–Mr. Merity. Attendance–5,500.

THE ATHLETICS AND PHILA. GIANTS

The Athletics were victorious, getting three men over the plate, while they held the Giants without a run. Rube Vickers was in the box for the Athletics, and the big fellow worked in mid-Summer style. He allowed but four hits, one of which was very scratchy. The Giants had three chances to score, but the required hit was never forthcoming, nor would the Athletics slip up on any fielding plays. They played errorless ball, Chief Bender being the particular star. Seybold distinguished himself in right field by nabbing a fly after leaping over a score of heads.

Buckner, too, did great work in the box, only four hits being made off his delivery. Two of these, both doubles, came in the third, and with a pair of errors gave the Athletics all their runs. After Peterson had died at first, Vickers pushed one to centre for two bases and scored when Hartsel dropped one in the crowd for a pair of cushions. Buckner fumbled Cross' bounder, Monte reaching first and Topsy taking third. After Cross had stole and Seybold had skied to Grant, Captain Davis raised a high one to right. Wilson dropped the ball and both runners counted.

Hill's work at short was the feature of the Giants' play, and Peterson and E. Wilson are deserving of special mention for clever fielding stunts. The score:

ATHLETICS

	R.	H.	O.	A.	E.
Hartsel, left field	1	2	1	0	0
Cross, short stop	1	0	4	0	0
Seybold, right field	0	1	1	0	0
Davis, first base	0	0	11	1	0
Nichols, third base	0	0	1	1	0
Bender, second base	0	0	0	7	0
Lord, centre field	0	0	0	0	0
Peterson, catcher	0	0	9	2	0
Vickers, pitcher	1	1	0	1	0
Totals	3	4	27	12	0

xDavis out, hit by batted ball.

PHILA. GIANTS

	R.	H.	O.	A.	E.
Grant, second base	0	1	2	1	0
James, left field	0	0	1	0	0
Buckner, pitcher	0	2	1	5	1
Bradley, catcher	0	0	2	0	0

R. Wilson, first base	0	0	11	0	0
Robinson, centre field	0	0	1	0	0
Francis, third base	0	0	2	1	1
J. Hill, short stop	0	0	2	5	0
E. Wilson, right field	0	1	1	0	1
Totals	0	4	x23	12	3

| Giants | 0 | 0 | 0 | 0 | 0 | 0 | 0 | 0 | 0–0 |
| Athletics | 0 | 0 | 3 | 0 | 0 | 0 | 0 | 0 | x–3 |

Two-base hits–Hartsel, 2; Vickers, Buckner, E. Wilson. Sacrifice hit–James. Stolen base–Cross. Double plays–Peterson, Davis and Nichols; Buckner, Hill and Wilson; Hill and Grant. Left on bases–Giants, 3; Athletics, 4. Struck out–By Vickers, 8; by Buckner, 2. Bases on balls–Off Vickers, 1; off Buckner, 2. Hit by pitched ball–Buckner. Time–75 minutes. Umpire–Wid Conroy, of the New York Americans.

Palm Beach, Fla., has been the Mecca for colored ball players during the Winter seasons. The two large hotels there giving them employment and the beautiful base ball grounds near the Royal Poinciana, the largest hotel in the world, affords them the opportunity of making a neat sum of money through the games played between teams representing the Poinciana and Breakers hotels.

F. Allen and Wm. Evans have been the headwaiters to promote base ball at this great Winter resort.

A. M. Thompson, now headwaiter of the Royal Palm Hotel, Miami, Fla., has entered the field and will place a fast colored team in Miami to represent the Royal Palm.

Seabreeze and Ormond are represented by white teams composed of American and National League players, and the contests between the colored boys of Palm Beach and the white boys from Ormond and Seabreeze are looked for yearly and draw immense crowds. Such players as Delehanty, McIntyre, Applegate and Wakefield of the American League; Ritchie, Needham and Dugan of the National League, play with Ormond and Seabreeze.

Of the four games played between the white and colored teams last Winter, the white boys failed to win a game.

The games resulted as follows:

February 14. –

| Seabreeze | 0 | 0 | 0 | 0 | 0 | 2 | 0 | 0 | 0 – 2 |
| Palm Beach | 0 | 0 | 2 | 0 | 0 | 0 | 0 | 0 | 1 – 3 |

Batteries–Dugan and Wakefield; Earl and Smith.

| Seabreeze | 0 | 0 | 0 | 0 | 2 | 0 | 1 | 0 | 0 | 0 | 0 | 0 – 3 |
| Palm Beach | 0 | 0 | 0 | 2 | 0 | 0 | 0 | 1 | 0 | 0 | 0 | 0 – 3 |

Batteries–Seabreeze, E. Dugan and Butler; Palm Beach, Buckner and Petway.

February 27. –

| Ormond | 0 | 0 | 0 | 1 | 1 | 0 | 0 | 0 | 0 – 2 |
| Palm Beach | 1 | 0 | 0 | 0 | 5 | 0 | 2 | 0 | x – 8 |

Batteries–Ormond, Applegate, Rudolph, Needham; Palm Beach–Earl and Smith.

February 28. –

| Ormond | 0 | 0 | 2 | 1 | 0 | 2 | 0 | 1 | 1 – 7 |
| Palm Beach | 0 | 2 | 2 | 0 | 0 | 3 | 2 | 0 | x – 9 |

Batteries–O. Ritchie and Needham; P. Beacon, Buckner and Johnson.

THE COLORED GIANTS.
A BRIEF SKETCH OF
TRENTON'S BASE CLUB

Trenton Times, *Trenton, Monday Afternoon, 10 May 1886*

The Men Who Will Represent This City in Base Ball the Present Season – Where They Have Played and the Results They Have Severally Made

Below will be found a brief sketch of the "Cuban Giants," the club which will represent this city during the present season. All the men comprising the club are fine players and have made good records with the various clubs they have played with during their careers as handlers of the "sphere."

Third baseman. B. F. Holmes was born in King and Queen county, Virginia, April 3, 1858, began playing baseball in his 18th year, has played with the famous colored Douglas club of Washington, D.C., covering 3d base in grand style, playing six games without an error, has played against the following clubs: Hartfords, Springfields, Nationals, Mets, Athletics, Holyokes, Westfields, has traveled east and west, is a fair batsman and good base runner, and now is playing with the Cuban Giants of Trenton.

Catcher No. 1. Arthur Thomas, born in Washington, December 10th, 1864, first caught for the Manhattan base ball club of Washington season '80, played in the same position for the West End base ball club of Long Branch in '81,-'82, and for the Cuban Giants in '85-'86. He is a good general playe[r], a good batsman, fair base runner, and excellent throw to bases.

Short stop. Benjamin Boyd was born April 8th, 1858, played 3d base for the Manhattan in 1874, 2d for the Mutuals in 1875, and short stop for the Cuban Giants in '84 and '85. He is a good general player, playing 3d, short stop and 2d base with great credit against the New York league team and Athletics of Philadelphia. He is a good batsman, and good base runner.

Right fielder, Geo. A. Parego was born in Charlottesville, Va., August 20th, 1861. First made his hit as a ball player with the Keystone Athletic of Philadelphia, as first and catcher, season of 1884, and played right field with great credit for the Cuban Giants the season of '85 and '86, making some very difficult catches, with great style and ease.

First baseman. Andrew G. Randolph was born in Philadelphia, November 14th, 1861, played '82 and '83 with the Active of Philadelphia as 1st baseman, '84 and '85 with the Resolutes of Boston, and traveled through the South with the Cuban Giants the winter of '86. He is an exceptional good baseman and fair batsman.

Catcher No. 2. Clarence Williams was born January 27th, 1886 [sic], at Harrisburg. Played left field for the Harrisburg's in '82, caught for the Middleton base ball club of Pennsylvania, in 1883, and played the same position for the Williamsport professionals in the early part of the season of '85, and joined the Cuban Giants the latter part of the season. He is a heavy batsman, fine base runner and good catcher.

Pitcher No. 1. Shepard Trusty was born in Philadelphia, May 10th, 1863, has played with the Millville, of N.J., and the Orion, of Philadelphia. As a pitcher he is a phenomena, being unquestionably the finest colored pitcher in the country, having pitched against the Philadelphia league club, and only six hits were made off him, the same being against the Mets of New York, who could only make a total of seven hits off him.

Left fielder. Wm. Whyte was born in Providence, April 10th, 1860, has played his position with the St. Louis Black Stockings to great credit; he also played with the Resolutes of Boston, as left fielder and change pitcher, and made some of the finest catches that ever was seen on the Boston grounds. He joined the Cuban Giants in the season of 1885, and traveled through the South with them during the winter season, and now is in excellent condition.

Center fielder. Richmond Robinson was born in Washington, April 1st, 1856, has played baseball with all the principal colored teams in the country. With the famous St. Louis Black Stockings in 1883, and '84–'85 with the Altoonas, and he is a general player, good base runner and heavy batter.

Second baseman. Harry A. Johnson was born at Burlington, May 1st, 1860, first came before the public as a ball player in 1883, signing with the Post Office club, then with the Department League of Washington, D.C. He is a second Dunlap, covering more ground than ever was seen by any colored 2d baseman on the road, fair batsman, good base runner, and expert thrower.

The above named players will positively appear and play on Wednesday, in the opening game. They are all signed and grounds leased for the season. Lovers of the game will be amply repaid by a visit to the grounds Wednesday.

THE "GIANTS" VICTORIOUS

The Game at Arctic Park, Long Island, Yesterday

The Cuban Giants, of Trenton, played yesterday at Arctic Park with the professional Acmas of Long Island, in the presence of 4,000 people defeating them with ease. They received the generous applause of the large assembly for their conduct, fine batting and fielding. They made themselves great favorites and have already been advertised to play next Sunday to a much larger assemblage. The Cuban Giants will then be represented by their full team, which will open here on Wednesday and represent the city of Trenton for the season. The following is the score:

CUBAN GIANTS

	R.	R.H.	P.O.	A.	E.
Williams, c	2	1	7	1	1
Boyd, ss	2	1	1	2	1
Holmes, 3b	2	1	3	2	2
Parago, rf	1	1	1	2	1
Thomas, lf	2	2	2	0	0
Vactor, p	2	2	0	6	1
Johnson, 2b	0	0	4	3	2

	R.	R.H.	P.O.	A.	E.
Shadney, cf	0	1	2	0	0
Randolph, 1b	0	2	8	0	0
Totals	11	11	27	16	8

ACMAS

	R.	R.H.	P.O.	A.	E.
Hender, 1b	1	0	9	0	1
Etting, lf	2	0	1	0	0
Chatham, p	0	0	2	5	1
McKennar, 3b	1	2	1	2	1
Cary, c	0	1	6	0	1
Cunningham, ss	0	1	2	3	0
Geidel, 2b	1	1	1	2	2
O'Neil, cf	0	1	1	0	1
Hallahan, rf	0	0	1	0	1
Total	5	6	24	12	8

INNINGS

	1	2	3	4	5	6	7	8	9	
Giants	1	2	1	0	5	0	0	2	x	– 11
Acmas	0	0	0	0	1	2	0	2	0	– 5

Two-base hits–Randolph, 1. Left on bases–Giants 4, Acmas 3. Struck out–by Vactor 6, by Chatham 5. Bases on balls–by Vactor 1, by Chatham 2. Passed balls–Williams 2, Cary 3. Wild pitches–Chatham 1. Time of game–2 hours and 15 minutes. Umpire–McLean.

4 THE CUBAN GIANTS . . .
J. Gordon Street,
Boston correspondent

New York Age, *15 October 1887*

The Cuban Giants, the great colored base ball nine, whose appearance in this city on Friday, Sept. 30, created such interest and enthusiasm, and whose magnificent playing called forth vociferous plaudits, has an interesting and creditable history which shall be known of all colored and white lovers of the national sport. That their record is a brilliant one no one will dispute after reading the following facts: Mr. F. P. Thompson, formerly of Philadelphia, but now of the Hotel Vendome, this city [Boston], organized, in May, 1885, in Philadelphia, the Keystone Athletics. On July 1, they were transferred to Babylon, L. I. During the month of August a consolidation of the Keystone Athletics, the Manhattans of Washington, D.C., and the Orions of Philadelphia, took place, under the name of the Cuban Giants. The proprietors were Messrs. F. P. Thompson, S. K. Govern and C. S. Massy.

The Cuban Giants' first series of games consisted of 26, 21 of which were victories. Their opponents were the Allentowns, the Hazeltons, the Williamsports, Lock [illegible; Havens?], Mahoney Cities, and all Pennsylvania State League Clubs, Athletics and Metropolitans of A.M.A. During the winter of '85 Thompson and Govern took the team for a tour through the entire South, finally locating in Florida, under the professional training of S. K. Govern. They played a series of games in every large city from St. Augustine to Philadelphia, with the honor of an unbroken string of victories – 40 games. They made a total of 116 runs to 14 made by their antagonists. They then located at Trenton, N.J. They won the first thirty-five games, played with the Bridgeport, Hartford, Long Island, Newark and Jersey City clubs of the Eastern League, also

Cincinnati and Kansas City of the National League. The Cuban Giants club was regularly incorporated before Judge Donohue in New York City, Oct. '86.

The personnel of the team is as follows: S. K. Govern, sole manager; Geo. W. Williams of Philadelphia, 2d base and captain; Arthur Thomas, Washington, catcher; Clarence Williams, Harrisburg, Pa., catcher; Wm. T. Whyte, Providence, R.I., pitcher; Wm. Selden, Boston, pitcher; Wm. Malone, Detroit, pitcher; H. A. Johnson, Washington, left field and catcher; John H. Frye, Harrisburg, 1st base; B. H. Holmes, Washington, 3d base; Abram Harrison, Philadelphia, short stop; George Parego, Lexington, Va., left field and pitcher; B. W. Boyd, Washington, center field.

The management will negotiate for Stovey, pitcher of the Newarks, and Brown of the Resolutes of Boston for the season of '88. S. K. Govern of St. Croix, W.I., will continue as manager. The present season will close about Oct. 23. The last games will be at Cincinnati, Oct. 22 and 23. The manager can be found during the Winter at the Coddington, 47 Buckingham street.

5 PREJUDICE ON THE DIAMOND: EVENTS OF THE SEASON AT ST. AUGUSTINE

S. K. Govern

New York Age, *23 February 1889*

Inaugurating a Course of Annual Sermons on Race Progress. The Detroit Base Ball Club to Play the Cuban Giants at Richmond

Special Correspondent of THE AGE
St. Augustine, Fla., Feb. 11. . . .
Mr. Wm. Cook of Trenton, N.J., brother of the late Walter I. Cook, proprietor of the Cuban Giants, took lunch at the Ponce de Leon last Friday. The Standards defeated the Cuban Giants on Friday by a score of 7 to 4. Thomas pitched and Malone caught for the Standard, Boyd and Catto being the battery for the Giants. Clarence Williams, the king of base ball coachers, is quite sick and will not be able to play for at least a couple of weeks. Frye's shoulder is well and he is putting up a great game at shortstop for the Standard. The report going the rounds of the papers that the Detroits have cancelled their games with the Cuban Giants at Richmond April 9 and 10 is incorrect. The Philadelphia *Record* stated that a number of citizens of Richmond requested Mr. R. H. Leadley to cancel the games, as they do not want colored and white clubs to play there against each other. But Mr. Leadley has ignored the request and assured me he has no intention of cancelling the games and sees no reason why he should. If there were a few more R. H. Leadleys in the profession, color prejudice would soon be a thing of the past in the South. . . .

Sporting News, *23 March 1889*

There are only four or five colored professional ball players who have gained any prominence on the diamond. What fame they have won has been made in the face of very disheartening circumstances. Race prejudice exists in professional base ball ranks to a marked degree, and the unfortunate son of Africa who makes his living as a member of a team of white professionals has a rocky road to travel.

The rest of the players not only cut him in a social way, but most of them endeavor to "job him" out of the business. He gets the wrong instructions in coaching, and when a field play came up in which he is interested an effort is always made to have an error scored against him.

The International League is about the only organization that gives employment to colored players. Fowler, the second baseman; Grant, of the Buffalos; Higgins, the pitcher; Walker, the catcher; and Stovey, colored players were all employed in different teams in that organization.

An International [League] player, talking to the writer the other day, said, "While I myself am prejudiced against playing in a team with a colored player, still I could not help pitying some of the poor black fellows that played in the International League. Fowler used to play second base with the lower part of his legs encased in wooden guards. He knew that about every other player that came down to second base on a steal had it in for him, and would, if possible, throw the spikes into him. He was a good player, but left the base every time there was a close play in order to get away from the spikes.

["]I have seen him muff balls intentionally, so that he would not have to try to touch runners, fearing that they might injure him. Grant was the same way. Why, the runners chased him off second base. They went down too often trying to break his legs or injure them, [so] that he gave up his infield position the latter part of last season and played right field. This is not all.

["]About half the pitchers try their best to hit these colored players when at the bat. I know of a great many pitchers that tried to soak Grant. . . . One of the International League pitchers pitched for Grant's head all the time. He never put a ball over the plate but sent them straight and true right at Grant. Do what he could he could not hit the Buffalo man, and he trotted down to first on called balls all the time.["]

7 NOWHERE SO SHARPLY DRAWN AS IN BASEBALL

Sporting Life, *11 April 1891*

Probably in no other business in America is the color line so finely drawn as in base ball. An African who attempts to put on a uniform and go in among a lot of white players is taking his life in his hands. Manager Cushman, of Milwaukee, in speaking of the item going the rounds of the Western press to the effect that he had signed Bruce Gordon, the colored second baseman, got telling about the experience a colored player had in the International League during 1887 when "Cush" was managing the Torontos. They were at Buffalo one day, and the latter team had an African named Grant playing second base. Early in the game Gus Alberts started out by hitting safely for first, and then shot down to second with the pitcher's arm. Grant squared away as the ball came down to him, and swinging about caught Gus in the pit of the stomach with his arm. Alberts was badly doubled up, but came in and said nothing. Ed Crane was looking at the play and said:

"Well, boys, what'll we do to him?"

"Put him out of the game," in a chorus.

This was agreed and when Crane went down to steal second Grant got squarely in front of him. Crane was going like the wind. He ducked his head after measuring the distance and caught Grant squarely in the pit of the stomach with his shoulder. The son of Ham went up in the air as if he had been in a thrashing machine. They took him home on a stretcher, and he didn't recover for three weeks.

"The crowd came near mobbing us," said Cush, "but there were no more darkies in the League after that."

8   BALLPLAYERS DO NOT BURN

[Quoting Ned Williamson on Frank Grant]

Sporting Life, 24 October 1891

Ballplayers do not burn with a desire to have colored men on the team. It is in fact the deep-seated objection to Afro-Americans that gave rise to the feet-first slide. Some go feet-first, others go head-first. Those who adopt the latter are principally those who served in the dark days before 1880. They learned the trick in the East. The Buffalos had a negro for second base. He was a few shades blacker than a raven, but was one of the best players in the Eastern [sic] League. The haughty Caucasians of the Association were willing to permit darkies to carry water to them or guard the bat bag, but it made them sore to have one of them in the line-up. They made a cabal and introduced new features into the game. The players of the opposing team made it a point to spike this brunett Buffalo. They would tarry at second when they might easily make third just to toy with the sensitive shins of this second baseman. The poor man played only two games out of five, the rest of the time he was on crutches. To give the frequent spiking an appearance [sic] he put wooden armor on his legs for protection, but the opposition proceeded to file their spike to a sharper point and split the cylinder. The colored man seldom lasted. The practice survived long after the second baseman had made his last trip to the baseplate, and this is how Kelly learned to slide.

STOVEY, THE PITCHER AND HIS EXPERIENCE IN JERSEY CITY - ANSON'S PREJUDICE

Cleveland Gazette, *13 February 1892*

Manager Powers, of the New York League club submitted to an interview recently, of which the following is a part: "During the season of 1886 Jersey City was fighting it out with the then very strong Newark team, and I struck a day that looked dark. Mike Tiernan's arm gave out, and I didn't have any one to put in the box.

"The next day we were to play Newark, and the championship depended on the game. So I had to do some tall thinking to decide upon a play to let the Jersey people down easy.

"By luck I happened to think to think of a colored pitcher named Stovey in Trenton, a fellow with a very light skin, who was playing on the Trenton team. It was my game to get him to Jersey City the next day in time for the game.

"I telegraphed a friend to meet me in Trenton at midnight, and went down to Stovey's house, roused him up, and got his consent to sign with Jersey City.

"Meanwhile some Trenton people got onto the scheme and notified the police to prevent Stovey from leaving town. I became desperate. I worked a member of 'Trenton's finest' all right, and finally hired a carriage, and, amid a shower of missiles, drove Stovey to a station below, where we boarded a train for Jersey City.

"I gave Stovey $20 to keep up his courage, and dressed him in a new suit of clothes as soon as the stores opened in the morning. I then put him to bed and waited for the game.

"When I marched my men on the field the public was surprised, and Tom Day, Tom Burns, Tucker, Greenwood, and 'Phenomenal' Smith, of the Newark team, gave me the laugh. Smith was then pitching his best game, and he went into the box. Stovey was put in to pitch for the home team, and dropped the Newarks out in one, two, three order.

"The game ended with the score 1 to 0 in Jersey City's favor, and Stovey owned the town.

"The same season the New York league team had a fighting chance to win from Chicago, and Walter Appleton of the New York club, was very much in favor of having Stovey sent to Chicago to pitch the last four decisive games. In fact, a deal was fixed between Appleton, the Jersey club, and Stovey to this end. Stovey had his grip packed and awaited the word, but he was not called owing to the fact that Anson had refused to play in a game with colored Catcher Walker at Toledo and the same result was fear.["]

Pittsburgh Courier, *12 March 1927*

ateline: New York, N.Y., March 10, 1927. If you were asked to name who you considered the greatest figures in colored baseball history, could you give an intelligent answer? I put this question to Sol White, organizer and manager of the Philadelphia Giants from 1902 to 1908, and this is his answer:

Old Timers	*Great Modernist*
Gos Govern, Cuban Giants	Rube Foster, American Giants
J. M. Bright, Cuban Giants	C. I. Taylor, Indianapolis
Walter Schlichter, Phila. Giants	A.B.C.s
Ambrose Davis, N.Y. Gorhams	Jess and Eddie McMahon,
Nat Strong, Promoter	Lincoln Giants
J. W. Connor, Brooklyn Royal	Jim Keenan, Lincoln Giants
Giants	Ed Bolden, Hilldale

That's Sol White's list. Sol, once-famous figure on the diamond and veteran manager, is now retired, living at 207 W. 140th street. He has been close to the game since its beginnings in 1885 and he hardly talks about anything else. The *Courier* representative was glad to find somebody who really knew the history of the game and was willing to talk. Sol has even written a history of the game. His "Sol White's History of Colored Baseball" appeared so long ago that there are ads in the back reading like this: "For a Bottle of Good 50¢ Whiskey Go to McGettigan's, 700 South 11th street, Philadelphia, Pa., Golden Age Whiskey a Specialty." That "50¢" sounds like ancient history in these parts.

Sol White (King Solomon White) was born at Bellaire, Ohio, June 27, 1868. His professional career began in 1887 when he went with the Keystones of Pittsburgh, then in the Colored National League. Other clubs in the league at that time were the Resolutes of

Boston, Lord Baltimore of Baltimore, Gorhams of New York, Washingtonians of Washington, Pythians of Philadelphia and the Louisvilles of Louisville. This was the first colored league in the United States and Walter Brown of Pittsburgh was President and Secretary. After a season with the Pittsburgh Keystones Sol joined the white Keystones of Wheeling, W. Va., as left field and later played second base. Next he went with the Wheelings, another white club of the Ohio League, then the Tri-State League, as third baseman. At the end of the season they drew the color line and that was the end of his career on big league white teams.

Bellaire, Ohio, where Sol was born, had three white teams, the Lillies, the Browns, and the Globes. As a boy Sol hung around the Globes and then came the time when the Globes had an engagement with the Marietta team. One of the Globe players got his finger smashed and since they all knew Sol, the captain pushed him into the game. Sol will always remember that game for the captain and second baseman of the Marietta team was none other Ban B. Johnson, in later years president of the American League and a leading sportsman of the West. Sol takes pride in having played against Ban when he was an obscure captain of a hick town club.

In 1888 the rule barring colored players in the Tri-State League was rescinded and Sol was sent to Lima to join the Wheeling team, then on the road, but the manager refused to use him. He then went back to the Pittsburgh Keystones and came to New York for the first time to compete for the silver ball offered by J. M. Bright, owner of the Cuban Giants. The teams competing were Hoboken, Long Island City, Norfolk Red Stockings, Gorhams, and Cuban Giants of New York as well as the Keystones.

Here we may begin a chronological story of Sol White's baseball career.

1889–With New York Gorhams as catcher, first and second base. Salary $10 per week and expenses.
1890–With J. M. Bright's Cuban Giants as left fielder part of season, Then went with J. Monroe Kreider's York, Pa., team as second baseman.
1891–Back with the Cuban Giants, behind in salary. Went with the

Hotel players, Palm Beach, Fla., early 1900s. In the 1890s black teams were formed to represent Palm Beach's two exclusive winter resort hotels, the Royal Poinciana and the Breakers. The Palm Beach association with African American baseball extended well into the 1920s, when Rube Foster's Chicago American Giants played for the Royal Poinciana against a collection of players from the east representing the Breakers. Courtesy The Historical Society of Palm Beach County.

Big Gorhams of New York owned by Ambrose Davis (also owner of regular Gorhams), both Gorhams that year managed by Cos Govern.

1892–Started with revived Pittsburgh Keystones awhile – dull year. Went to Hotel Champlain at Bluff Point, N.Y., under same head-waiter who started Cuban Giants (Frank P. Thompson) and played on Hotel Team.

1893–From first of season to June with Boston Monarchs, Al Jupiter, manager, then back with Cuban Giants, New York.

1894–With Cuban Giants.

Sol White : 145

1895–With Fort Wayne, Ind., Western Inter-State League team (white) as second baseman, $80 per month. League disbanded in June; joined Page Fence Giants, Adrian, Mich., $75 per month and expenses (a colored team) as second baseman. The name "Page Fence" was from the man who invented wire fences for farms.

1896–With Cuban Giants.

1897–With Cuban X-Giants. These players broke away from J. M. Bright's Cuban Giants because they didn't like his methods. They got a Frenchman, E. B. LeMar, to act as manager. LeMar was not a sportsman, but merely a follower. His job was principally that of bookkeeping. The men were guaranteed $80 per month in the cooperative plan. Sol played second base. The "Co" plan (as the cooperative plan was popularly known) was a system whereby all expenses were deducted from the gross receipts and the balance evenly distributed between the players.

1898, 1899, with Cuban X-Giants.

1900–Short stop with Columbia Giants, Chicago, John Patterson, manager.

1901–Back to New York with Cuban X-Giants.

1902–Organized the Philadelphia Giants and was captain and manager. Was associated in this venture with Walter Schlichter (white) sports editor of the Philadelphia Item, a daily paper, who was booker. First year on a co-operative plan. Cuban X-Giants main rivals. Played in Pennsylvania and New York. Uneventful season.

1903–Reorganized Giants and put men on salary; used big league plan and paid them from $60 to $90 per month. Brought in Harry Buckner, Chicago. William Binga, John Patterson, Bob Footes. Branched out and got into Atlantic City for games where Cuban X-Giants had kept them out season before. Got in Independent League composed of Harrisburg, Williamsport, Altoona, Lancaster (all white clubs) and Cuban X-Giants. Made good and paid well. Sol played shortstop first year and second base second year. In 1903 Rube Foster was on rival Cuban X-Giants.

1904–Changed personnel. Got Andrew Rube Foster and paid $90

per month as pitcher. Played white teams at 186th street and 5th Avenue in New York, bought by McMahon brothers (Eddie and Jess). Also played Edgewood and Long Island clubs at Brighton oval.

1905 – Changed line-up to strongest organization of the time. Kept Rube Foster and brought in "Home Run" Johnson as short stop. White clubs of the Independent League joined organized baseball. This year the Philadelphia Giants played several games in New England against the New England League (white) and never lost a game. Also played the Newark International League Team, then under the management of Ed. Barrow, now secretary of the New York Yankees. Beat the International Leaguers four games straight.

1906 – Changes. "Home Run" left to manage Brooklyn Royal Giants for John W. Connor. Jess McMahon started Philadelphia Quaker Giants and raided Philadelphia Giants and got Will Monroe and Chappie Johnson. Nat Harris of Chicago took "Home Run's" place as short stop and Bill Francis took Monroe's place on third base.

1907 – Got John Henry Lloyd, Willie James, Bruce Petway, Geo. Washington (pitcher) G. A. Rabbitt and Ashby Dunbar to replace old men who left.

1908 – Got Duncan, fielder, Fisher, pitcher, Hayman, pitcher. This was the last season of the club under Sol. Schlichter took club over.

1909 – Philadelphia Quaker Giants under McMahon disbanded. Sol strung along with his old team.

1910 – Managed Connor's Brooklyn Royal Giants.

1911 – Organized Lincoln Giants for McMahon brothers, and took job as manager. Left early in season.

1912 – Organized Boston Giants in New York. Went thru season but business was dull. Went home to Bellaire, O., late in season and retired from game until 1920.

1920 – Got Rube Foster to put team in Columbus, O., in Western (Negro National) League. Was secretary of the "Buckeyes" of Columbus to 1924.

1924–Managed Cleveland Browns in Western (Negro National) League. Disbanded same season.

1926–Assisted Andrew Harris coach Newark team. (NOTE: Newark Stars of the Eastern Colored League.)

Although the game in many reports treated him rough, Sol has only the best of wishes for it. He admits that in the heyday of his glory of 1905, 06, and 07 (the latter year the one in which he published his history) he was high strung, still he is a calm, quiet man now who likes to go to the library and read good books when he is not at work. His object in telling his story is to let some of the younger fellows know something of what is behind them – something of the struggles that have made possible the improved conditions of the present. He can tell of many times when his men were on the "Co" plan how he gave up all his money in order to keep his players together. Some owners went into the game to make money, and made it, but Sol takes greater pride in having watched the game develop to where it is today, although he has no money to show for it. He has a new book he would like to publish, a kind of second edition to his old one, bringing the game from 1907 down to date, and if there is anybody anywhere in sports circles who thinks enough of what has been before to help Sol print his record, he will be glad to hear from them. Without a doubt this record will prove valuable in years to come. Sol's personal copy of his own book is the only he knows about and it would be a historical tragedy if this should be lost.

11 THE GRAND OLD GAME
Sol White

(New York) Amsterdam News, *18 December 1930*

A s it is our purpose at this time to give the readers of The Amsterdam News names of men of the early days whom we judge contributed largely to the growth of baseball and a few of the noted stars of the diamond who, prior to the organization of the first professional colored team, the Cuban Giants, were considered among the greatest players of the time, we will have to omit the names of quite a number of individuals and many incidents during the life of the sport that would be interesting to old-time fans and no doubt excite the curiosity of its followers in the present day.

As a matter of fact, there could be no baseball team without any baseball players. The Cuban Giants were recognized as a full-fledged professional team in 1886. From whence the players came and who they were that composed the Cuban Giants at that time is a story too extensive for elaboration in this article. All that we will state for the time being is that Washington, D.C., and Philadelphia, Pa., were the main contributors to the personnel of the country's first colored professional baseball team.

With the backing of Mr. Walter Cook, a capitalist of Trenton, N.J., and a ground well equipped and adequate for all purposes, the Cuban Giants started their career under the most auspicious conditions. During the seasons of 1886 and 1887 they met every big league team in the country, with the exception of the St. Louis Browns, and held their own with all of them.

While the Cuban Giants were making a wonderful reputation as an aggregation of colored ball players, at times they were meeting teams having in their line-ups some of the greatest Negro players in the history of the game, who were playing on different teams of the International League. Fleet Walker, George Stovey, Frank Grant,

Bud Fowler, Tobe Higgins and Renfro were members of white teams that visited the Cuban Giants at Trenton.

The great success of the Giants was an inducement for several large cities to organize teams and form an association to be called the "Negro National League," which was in 1887. It was a great effort on the part of the promoters, but it fizzled out before the schedule of the first month was finished.

The death of Mr. Cook in 1888 put the Cuban Giants into the hands of J. M. Bright (white) and Cos Govern (colored). Govern, who had managed the Giants while they were under the ownership of Mr. Cook, was a smart fellow and a shrewd baseball man. J. M. Bright at that time was a lover of the game and a money-getting baseball man. We class Bright as the leading spirit of his day in keeping the game before the public. Ambrose Davis, owner of the Gorham baseball team of New York and the first colored man in the East to venture into professional baseball, proved to be of great assistance to the game by his competitiveness in producing teams to combat the great Cuban Giants. The Gorhams was the first colored team to beat the Cuban Giants in the early stages of the game. That feat was accomplished in an exhibition game between the two teams in Newburgh, N.Y., in 1887. The next colored team to conquer the Cuban Giants was the Keystones, of Pittsburgh, in 1887. The Keystones in the latter part of 1887 and the fall season of '88 were the runners-up in baseball to the Cuban Giants. In the tournament of 1888, in competition with the Cuban Giants, Gorhams of New York, and the Red Stockings of Norfolk, Va., for a silver cup donated by J. M. Bright, the Keystones were beaten by the Cuban Giants only. They won every game played against the Gorhams and the Red Sox.

But we started this article for the express purpose of giving you an honest personal opinion of men that have been in the game as owners or otherwise and men who have played a part in keeping the game alive and have shown concern for its future.

Of "ye olden-time" owners of colored baseball teams we would place J. M. Bright, second owner of the Original Cuban Giants, at the head of all men who dabbled in the game. "J.M.," as he was called by his players, was extremely selfish in his financial dealings and naturally shrewd. Whether under salary or working on the coplan, his players were always called upon to help him in an idea. When it came to getting money, "J.M." was full of ideas. He held up many games after his team reached a ground with a packed stand and demanded a boost in his stipulated guarantee. He generally got what he asked for. Bright spent his life in colored baseball, and he was not a millionaire when he died.

In 1896 the veteran ball players who had been playing under Bright for several years launched out on their own initiative. They secured E. B. Lamar, Jr., as booking agent and manager. Lamar is another one of the early baseball men who spent his time and mind in making the game a lucrative calling for ball players. Lamar was manager and booking agent for the Cuban Giants from 1895 to 1906, inclusive. His efforts were in the interest of his team, and he was held in the highest regard by the players.

Walter Schlichter, the man who was the instigator of the original Philadelphia Giants, was my ideal of an owner of a colored baseball team. "Slick," as he was called, was a sportsman and a business man. As the saying goes, "he was a man after my own heart." A swimmer, boxer, boat puller, sprinter, a manager of boxing clubs and boxers, his attitude toward ball players was from the standpoint of athletics. In our association with him as manager of his baseball team, every player that joined the Philadelphia Giants, athletically speaking, was analyzed from the crown of his head to the soles of his feet. When it came to the business part of the game, Schlichter was "Slick." He knew his manager. J. W. Connor was the second race man to gain prominence as an owner of a professional ball club. Mr. Connor played a noble part in keeping the game before the public. Like all true baseball men, he loved the game and went the limit for the "grand old sport."

We have mentioned some of the men who, as owners and managers, have contributed largely to the advancement of baseball from 1886 to 1905. There are others who have been identified with the game and did their bit in the interest of the sport, but like the proverbial old cow, "They filled the pail, and kicked it over."

While the East was coming along with its baseball activities, out in the West the old game was only a stride or two behind their eastern brethren. Indeed, if it came to honors being conferred on the first colored team of note, although not a professional baseball club, the Black Diamonds of St. Louis, Mo., would have to be conceded the palm. They were given considerable publicity by the white press of the country as far back as 1884. The next prominent team in the West was formed in Lincoln, Neb., in 1890, which was the first colored professional team in that section of the country. Next we hear of Will Peters and Frank Leland with the famous Chicago Unions and Messrs. Hoch and Parsons, backers of the noted "Page Fence Giants," of Adrian, Mich., 1895; the Columbia Social Club of Chicago that backed the noted Columbia Giants, 1899–1900. We like the efforts of Will Peters and Frank Leland in trying to advance the game. Their long and continuous participation in the sport surely gives them a high rating in the ranks of pioneers of baseball.

Passing over owners and teams that were in existence between 1895 and 1919 we come to the part of colored baseball history that has to do with the big colored leagues.

The first league of modern times was formed in 1919 or 1920 with Chicago, Detroit, Kansas City, St. Louis, Indianapolis, Dayton, Ohio, with the Cuban Stars as members of the organization. The late C. L. Taylor and Andrew "Rube" Foster were the leading spirits of the association. Back of the league was the unanimous support of the Negro press throughout the country. Rube Foster was selected as president, secretary-treasurer, chairman of the Board of Directors and schedule maker. During the first season of the league every team in the organization made money. After the initial season there has been yearly changes in the make-up of its membership until the present day.

A few years after the West had started a coalition of baseball teams, as set forth in the above paragraph, colored teams of the East banded together and formed an association similar to the so-called "Negro National League." Lincoln Giants and Royal Giants of New York, Hilldale of Philadelphia, Potomacs of Washington D.C.; Bacharachs of Atlantic City, Baltimore Black Sox, Harrisburg, Pa., and Cuban Stars. Here we have two men, since a league started in the East, that have shown a true interest in the advancement and preservation of the game. Ed Bolden, of the Hilldale team of Philadelphia, has worked from the ground up in the business end of the game. He has given people of his home city some of the greatest ball playing of all times, and a home ground for his players. James Keenan, owner of the Lincoln Giants, has placed his team on Catholic Protectory grounds as a home attraction. There is no other ground in Greater New York that can be named as "home grounds" for a colored baseball team. During the many years the Lincoln Giants have been stationed at Protectory Oval under the ownership of James Keenan, along with Hilldales, they were the highest salaried colored team in the country. Keenan has had strong opposition here in New York, but he has fought a good fight. There is not a well-wisher of the game that does not trust and hope for the Lincoln Giants to continue their sojourn under the present ownership at Protectory Oval.

I have given you just a sketch of what has happened in days of the past in baseball. You should know something about the present. From a sport baseball has changed to a commercialized activity. To my mind the shift was rather premature for the good of colored baseball. As a business proposition it fell into the hands of men who had lost all the love they ever had for the game. They grabbed the reins and rode into power before the game had developed sufficiently to endure their corrupt methods of commercialized baseball, consequently the game today is far below the standard hoped for by the hard-working men of the past who gave their time and energy to its advancement.

We claim, and we are not alone in the assertion, that the colored press has played a big part in shaping the course of the game in late years. If baseball has veered towards the shoals of business inactiveness and sloth, let the press put it on the right course and bring it up to where it belongs – one of the greatest institutions of the race.

New York Age, *20 December 1930*

One summer's evening, not so many years ago, I and several other fellows found ourselves on the streets of a small town in the State of Ohio with lots of time to spend, but how and where to spend such a valuable commodity in a town of a few thousand souls, a city hall and two colored churches was a question among the gang with each and every body of the bunch at variance as to where to go and what to do to while away the hours. With no agreement imminent the boys were making preparations to hike to the station and spend the time listening to crickets' songs while waiting for the train. At the moment, along comes a native son of this lonesome municipality and extends an invitation to the bunch urging our attendance at a lecture to be held in one of the colored churches. Of course we all went to the church and took our baggage with us and listened to the lecture on "Progress of the Negro." The lecturer went away back into the history of the world and told of many wars in which the Negro had shed his blood for justice and his race; he spoke of Commodore Perry and his conquest of the North Pole in very impressive language. At the conclusion of every citation in which the Negro was mentioned as playing an heroic part the lecturer, in a forceful voice, would say, "And the Negro, he was in it." We did enjoy the lecture but the climax of the evening's entertainment came when one of the boys said, "He never said anything about the Big League; they've been Negroes in that too."

The first scheme for playing baseball was devised by a gentleman in Cooperstown, N.Y., back in 1839. The first Negro ballplayers of prominence was Bud Fowler. We heard of Bud when, as a little tot, we were watching a ball game on the public square of my home town. Fowler passed the home plate many years ago. We never learned the exact age of Bud, but it wouldn't take such a ridiculous range of imagination to place Fowler somewhere in the neighborhood of Cooperstown when the first diamond for playing the old game was devised. You see? Bud was playing ball when I was a kid.

The Cuban Giants, first professional colored team, was a good one. They were stationed in Trenton, N.J. With good backing, in the person of Walter Cook, a Trenton capitalist and a colored manager by the name of Cos Govern. Their home grounds were not very large but what it lacked in space was offset in beauty. The Cubes had two great catchers at that time: Arthur Thomas and Clarence Williams. Speaking of Arthur Thomas, we will not hesitate in telling you that we never met a ballplayer with a similar disposition. He was 6 feet 4 inches in height; his arms almost reached his knees, he was sorta sway-backed and gangled-legged, he had a moaning voice and actually would cry when his team lost a game. His facial expressions were paradoxical; when he laughed you would have to look twice to see whether he was crying. An extremely hard worker, he ruled the roost including the captain. Thomas was a great receiver behind the bat. With his long arms he would reach out and grab wild pitches and when the ball left his hand for second base it looked like a long snake. We don't know how Arthur would take with the players of today but, there is one thing I do know, that is, a player with the earnestness of Arthur Thomas would make a hit with the fans.

Why don't "gentlemen of the press" look into this proposition that we hear so much whispering about? If a race team under the ownership and management of race men did secure the Yankee Stadium for their home games the venture is worthy of the heartiest support of press and public. What has been the main draw-back in the advancement of race baseball is contact. One of the greatest opening and opportunity for the advancement of the game is knocking at our door. There were some big doings at the Yankee Stadium the past season, it would be far greater next season. We hope Mr. Lancaster will retain his interest and gain the support of a few New York sportsmen and give us games at the Stadium next summer.

18 July 1936

Mr. Sol White
145 West 132nd Street
New York City, N.Y.
My Dear Sol: –

I am certainly glad to hear from you and to know that you are
doing well. It is indeed a pleasure to know that at least some of us
old timers are still able to "carry on." And, I know that you are in
your element at the Yankee Stadium and mixing with such baseball
history makers as Welch and Latham. I do not know Welsh [*sic*] but
I did know Arlie and he probably might rem[em]ber me. I was on
the old Item when he was in his prime.

It is true that I might have "made a million" or less had I stuck to
colored base ball but I doubt it. Outside of Nat Strong I know of no
one who has. And, at that, I am better off than he is right now. I am
still living and have my health and Nat didn't take his wealth with
him. There is no pocket in a shroud, you know.

I am [w]riting a weekly story for the Inquirer under the caption,
The Old Philadelphian and it pays enough for me to get along on. I
also am working on several other writing projects which I hope to
market to a good advantage, so I am kept pretty busy.

My delay in answering you was caused by the fact that my wife,
the second one, you know, has suffered a severe attack of arthritis
and, as she and I are alone, it takes considerable of my time to wait
on her and try to make her more comfortable.

As for the book, Sol, I have only two left and you will find one of
them enclosed. The other one I will not part with at any price so, if
that one will serve your purpose, you are welcome to it. I also have
all the cuts and photographs of the reproductions in the book and,
here is a suggestion. Why not see the Editor of your colored paper
and try to sell him a history of colored baseball which you could

write either as a single article or as a series. Except for recent years you have all the data in the book and I would be glad to furnish the cuts and pictures. It looks to me to be worth trying.

Wishing you continued health, wealth and prosperity, I am,

very sincerely yours,

[H. Walter Schlichter]

14. KING SOLOMON "SOL" WHITE CHRONOLOGY
Dick Clark

Year	Team	League	Position
1887	Pittsburgh Keystones	LCBBP	2b, lf
1887	Washington Capital Citys	LCBBP	2b, of
1889	Philadelphia New York Gorhams	Mid. States	1b, 2b, 3b
1890	York Cuban Giants	E. Interstate	1b, 2b, 3b
1891	New York Big Gorhams		1b, 2b
1891	Ansonia Cuban Giants	Conn. State league	1b, 3b
1893	Cuban Giants		2b
1895	Adrian (Mich.) Page Fence Giants		2b
1896	Cuban X-Giants		1b, 2b
1896	Cuban Giants		2b
1898	Cuban X-Giants		1b, 2b
1899	Cuban X-Giants		1b
1900	Chicago Columbia Giants		1b, ss
1902	Philadelphia Giants		1b, ss
1903	Philadelphia Giants		1b
1904	Philadelphia Giants		1b
1905	Philadelphia Giants		1b
1906	Philadelphia Giants		1b
1907	Philadelphia Giants		mgr, 1b
1909	Quaker Giants		2b, of
1924	Cleveland Browns		mgr

Source: Dick Clark, Negro League Committee, SABR.

Statistics:

Pos	Yrs	G	AB	R	H	2B	3B	HR	SB	BA
White, Sol										
2, 3	5	152	644	169	231	40	12	7	41	.359

Source: "Minor League Career Batting Records, 19th Century Black Players," by Bob Davids, SABR.

MINOR LEAGUE CAREER RECORDS OF SOME OF THE BEST BLACK PLAYERS OF THE 19TH CENTURY
Bob Davids

Batters (ranked by average)

	Pos.	Yrs	G	AB	R	H	2B	3B	HR	SB	BA
George Williams	Inf.	2	108	454	124	167	27	11	2	69	.368
Sol White	2-3	5	152	644	169	231	40	12	7	41	.359
Arthur Thomas	3-C	2	120	497	138	171	41	10	4	44	.344
Frank Grant	2-3	6	458	1879	410	634	123	34	31	149	.337
Bud Fowler	2-P	10	465	2039	455	628	112	38	7	190	.308
Abe Harrison	S-O	2	111	403	104	123	23	9	4	54	.305
Clarence Williams	C-O	3	102	420	98	126	17	3	1	41	.300
William Selden	P-O	2	124	474	94	140	14	8	2	47	.295
Richard Johnson	C-O	4	337	1471	297	398	63	29	14	130	.271
Ben Boyd	OF	3	102	408	85	107	8	2	1	46	.266
George Stovey	P-O	6	122	464	68	121	16	3	1	28	.261
Jack Frye	1-C	5	124	446	87	113	23	7	3	27	.253
Moses Walker	C-O	5	354	1295	215	293	27	15	4	100	.226

Pitchers (ranked by winning percentage)

	Yrs	G	IP	W		L	Pct.	H	R	BB	SO
William Whyte	2	49	421	37	-	10	.787	386	200	75	164
William Selden	2	53	451	39	-	11	.780	376	226	154	211
Robert Higgins	2	54	473	37	-	14	.725	465	280	107	207
George Stovey	6	102	882	60	-	40	.600	814	495	228	387

Compiled by Bob Davids with the assistance of members of the Society for American Baseball Research (SABR), this originally appeared in the *Bud Fowler Memorial Project Booklet.*

16 CHRONOLOGICAL REGISTRY OF 19TH-CENTURY BLACK PLAYERS IN ORGANIZED BASEBALL
Bob Davids

1878   *International Association*
John (Bud) Fowler, pitcher, Lynn, Mass. (3 games)

New England Association
John (Bud) Fowler, pitcher, Worcester, Mass.
  (pitched 1 game)

1883   *Interstate Association*
Jack Frye, first base, outfield, Reading, Pa.

Northwestern League
Moses F. Walker, catcher, Toledo, Ohio

1884   *American Association* (major league)
Moses F. Walker, catcher, Toledo, Ohio
Weldy W. Walker, outfield, second base, Toledo, Ohio

Northwestern League
John "Bud" Fowler, second base, pitcher, Stillwater, Minn.

1885   *Western League*
John "Bud" Fowler, second base, Keokuk, Iowa
Moses F. Walker, catcher, Cleveland, Ohio

Eastern League
Moses F. Walker, catcher, Waterbury, Conn.

Colorado League
John (Bud) Fowler, second base, pitcher, Pueblo

1886   *Western League*
John (Bud) Fowler, second base, Topeka, Kans.

Eastern League
George Stovey, pitcher, outfield, Jersey City, N.J.
Moses F. Walker, catcher, Waterbury, Conn.

Frank Grant, second base, Meriden, Conn.

International Association
Frank Grant, second base, Buffalo, N.Y.

Pennsylvania State Association
Jack Frye, first base, outfield, Lewistown, Pa.
Josh Herbert, catcher, Danville, Pa.

1887 *International League*
John "Bud" Fowler, second base, Binghamton, N.Y.
Frank Grant, second base, Buffalo, N.Y.
Robert Higgins, pitcher, Syracuse, N.Y.
Randolph Jackson, second base, Oswego, N.Y. (5 games)
William Renfro, pitcher, Binghamton, N.Y.
George Stovey, pitcher, outfield, Newark, N.J.
   (won 34 games)
Moses F. Walker, catcher, Newark, N.J.

Ohio State League
Richard Johnson, catcher, outfield, Zanesville
N. Higgins, catcher, Columbus
Weldy Walker, outfield, Akron
Sol White, second base, third base, Wheeling, W.V.

Central Interstate League
Richard Johnson, catcher, outfield, Springfield, Peoria, Ill.

Vermont League
John "Bud" Fowler, second base, pitcher, Montpelier
   (hit .425 in 7 games)

Northern Michigan League
Alex Ross, third base, Greenville

1888 *International Association*
Frank Grant, second base, outfield, Buffalo, N.Y.
Robert Higgins, pitcher, Syracuse, N.Y.
Moses F. Walker, catcher, Syracuse, N.Y.

Northeastern League
George Stovey, pitcher, Worcester, Mass.

Tri-State League
Richard Johnson, outfield, Zanesville, Ohio

Central Interstate League
John "Bud" Fowler, second base, Crawfordsville,
  Terre Haute, Ind.

New Mexico League
John "Bud" Fowler, second base, pitcher, Santa Fe

1889   *International Association*
Moses F. Walker, catcher, Syracuse, N.Y.

Michigan State League
John "Bud" Fowler, second base, Greenville
Alex Ross, third base, outfield, Greenville

Illinois-Indiana League
Arthur Grace, pitcher, first base, Champaign, Ill.
R. A. Kelly, infield, Danville, Ill.

Colorado State League
William Castone, pitcher, outfield, Aspen
George Taylor, catcher, infield, outfield, Aspen

Middle States League
Cuban Giants, Trenton, N.J. (all-black team)
  Ben Boyd, outfield
  Jack Frye, first base, pitcher
  Frank Grant, second base
  Abe Harrison, shortstop
  Ben Holmes, third base
  William H. Malone, pitcher, first base
  Harry Johnson, outfield
  John Nelson, pitcher, outfield
    (also New York Gorhams)
  George Parego, outfield
  William H. Seldon, pitcher, outfield
  George Stovey, pitcher, outfield (also New York
    Gorhams)

Arthur Thomas, first base, outfield
Shep Trusty, pitcher, outfield
William T. Whyte, pitcher, outfield
Clarence Williams, catcher, third base
George Williams, first base, third base

New York Gorhams, Philadelphia (all-black team)
Frank Bell, outfield
Harry Cato, second base, pitcher, outfield
Chamberlin, first base
Emory, catcher
Nat Collins, pitcher
Ross Garrison, shortstop
Andrew Jackson, third base
Oscar Jackson, outfield
Frank Miller, pitcher
John Nelson, pitcher, outfield (also Cuban Giants)
George Stovey, pitcher, outfield (also Cuban Giants)
Sol White, second base, third base

1890   *Eastern Interstate League*
Monarchs, York, Pa. (all-black team)
Ben Boyd, outfield
Jack Frye, first base, pitcher
Ross Garrison, shortstop
Good, outfield
Abe Harrison, shortstop
Andrew Jackson, third base
Oscar Jackson, outfield
William Jackson, catcher, second base, outfield
William H. Malone, pitcher, third base
William H. Selden, pitcher, outfield
W. W. Terrill, utility man
Arthur Thomas, catcher, first base
Sol White, second base, third base
William T. Whyte, pitcher, outfield
George Williams, first base, third base

Frank Grant, second base, outfield, Harrisburg
Clarence Williams, catcher, third base, shortstop,
　Harrisburg

Central Interstate League
John "Bud" Fowler, second base, Galesburg, Ill.
Richard Johnson, catcher, outfield, Peoria, Ill.

Illinois-Iowa League
John "Bud" Fowler, second base, Sterling, Ill., Galesburg,
　Ill., Burlington, Iowa

NY-Penn League
R. A. Kelly, infield, Jamestown, N.Y.

New York State League
George Stovey, pitcher, Troy (1–1 in 2 games)

1891　*Connecticut State League*
Cuban Giants, Ansonia (all-black team)
　Frank Bell, shortstop
　Ben Boyd, outfield
　Brown, outfield (probably Charles or William H.)
　Cam, outfield
　Douglas, outfield, pitcher (probably George)
　Evans, first base (probably George or John)
　Jack Frye, first base, pitcher
　Frank Grant, second base
　Bob Jackson, outfield
　William Jackson, second base, outfield
　John Nelson, pitcher, outfield
　George Stovey, pitcher, outfield
　W. W. Terrill, second base
　Sol White, third base
　William Whyte, pitcher
　Clarence Williams, catcher
　Woods, third base

New York-Penn League
R. A. Kelly, infield, Jamestown, N.Y.

1892   *Nebraska State League*

William Castone, pitcher, outfield, Lincoln-Kearney
John "Bud" Fowler, second base, Lincoln-Kearney
Frank Maupin, catcher, third base, Plattsmouth
John Reeves, third base, Plattsmouth
John Patterson, second base, Plattsmouth
George Taylor, first base, Beatrice
Ben Holmes, third base, Fremont

California League

Wilds, catcher, Stockton (played 1 game on 19 October)

1893   None

1894   *New England League*

Herbert, outfield, Pawtucket, R.I. (batted .250 in 10
    games, 7–17 May)
James Robinson, pitcher, outfield, Pawtucket, R.I. (1–1
    in 2 games as pitcher, 28 April and 5 May)

1895   *Michigan State League*

William Binga, catcher, Adrian (3 games)
Pete Burns, catcher, Adrian (4 games)
John (Bud) Fowler, second base, third base, Adrian,
    Lansing (.331 in 31 games)
Vasco Graham, catcher, Adrian (.324 in 77 games)
Joe Miller, pitcher, Adrian (1–0 in 1 game)
George H. Wilson, pitcher, outfield, Adrian (29–4 as
    pitcher)

Western Inter-State League

Sol White, second base, third base, Fort Wayne, Ind.

Kansas State League

Bert Wakefield, first base, second base, Emporia

1896   *Kansas State League*

Bert Wakefield, first base, second base, Emporia
Bert Jones, pitcher, outfield, Atchison

Colorado State League
> George Taylor, first base, outfield, catcher, Denver

1897 *Kansas State League*
> Bert Jones, pitcher, outfield, Atchison

1898 *Kansas State League*
> Bert Jones, pitcher, outfield, Atchison
> Bert Wakefield, second base, Salina

> *Iron and Oil League*
> *Celeron, N.Y.* (all-black team)
>> Al Baxter, outfield
>> Billy Booker, second base
>> Eddie Day, shortstop
>> George Edsall, outfield
>> William Kelly, third base
>> John Mickey, pitcher
>> William Payne, outfield
>> John Southall, catcher
>> Walter Williams, pitcher
>> Edward Wilson, pitcher
>> Clarence Wright, first base

1899 *Canadian League*
> Bill Galloway, outfield, Woodstock, Ont. (5 games,
> batting average .150)

A NOTE ON MILTON DABNEY, 1867-1967

The photos used in chapter 1, "Sol White's Official Base Ball Guide: History of Colored Base Ball," are reproduced from a copy of the original White guide belonging to (John) Milton Dabney's daughter-in-law, Lillian Dabney. Dabney had played on the 1885 Argyle Hotel team, then moved to the Cuban Giants (1885–86), ending his career with the Cuban X-Giants in 1896.

The Dabney family history is traceable to Dabney's paternal grandparents, London and Eliza Dabney, in antebellum Richmond, Virginia, and is rich with other notable members. Dabney's father, John, was a successful Richmond businessman after the Civil War. A brother, Wendell P. Dabney, owned the Cincinnati *Union* and published a book, *Cincinnati's Colored Citizens*.

Dabney returned to Richmond after his baseball career, eventually retiring from the U.S. Postal Service. On his ninety-ninth birthday, Dabney was asked the secret of his long life: "I never took a drink in my life, and never smoked, but I don't want to make it sound too good or I'll feel a pain in my back when the wings begin to sprout." He died in New Jersey four days before his one-hundredth birthday.

Lawrence D. Hogan

Binga, William: with Chicago Co-
lumbia Giants (1899), 28; with
Page Fence Giants (1895, '99),
24; with Philadelphia Giants
(1903, 1906–7), 40, 121, 123, 146
Binghamton NY, xix
Bluff Point NY, xxxi, 145
Bolden, Ed (owner, Hilldale Club,
Philadelphia) (1920s), 143, 152–
53
Booker, James ("Pete"), with Philadelphia Giants (1905–6), 75,
89
Boston, American League, xxxvi
Boston MA, xxiv, 12, 24
Boston Giants. *See* New York
Boston Giants
Boston Resolutes (1887), xxiii, 12,
131, 135, 143–44
Bowman, Emmett ("Scotty"), 65,
73, 118; with Philadelphia Gi-
ants (1904–7), 58, 89, 121, 123–
26
Boyd, Benjamin ("Ben"), *23*, 111;
early career, 130–31; minor
league statistics, 161; with
Cuban Giants (1885–88), *xxiii,
xxv*, 8, 10, 12, 130, 132, 135, 136;
with Monarchs of York (1890),
xxvii; with Philadelphia Orions
(1885), lxi
Bradley, Phil, with Brooklyn
Royal Giants (1907), 122, 125,
127–28
Breakers Hotel team, Palm Beach
FL, 145; in 1907, 128; in 1914,
xlv
Bridgeport CT, 10, 54, 134
Bright, John M. ("J.M.," owner,
Cuban Giants), *29*, 143; in 1888,
14, 16, 143, 150; in 1890, xxvi–
xxviii, 18, 20; in 1891, xxviii,
xxx; in 1892, 24; in 1896, xxxv–
xxxvi; in 1897, 146; White's assessment of, 150–51
Brighton Athletic Club, Brooklyn
NY (1906), 33

Brighton Oval, Brooklyn NY
(1906), 33, 147
Brooklyn, National League, xlvi
Brooklyn NY, xxxvi, xlviii, 31, 91
Brooklyn Royal Giants, 18, 65, 74,
143; of 1906, xxxix, xli, xlvii, 31,
33, 46, *80*; of 1907, 121–25; of
1908, 120; of 1920s, 152
Brooks, Gus, with Page Fence Gi-
ants (1895), 24
Brown, Walter S. (founder,
League of Colored Base Ball
Players) (1887), xxii, 12, 144
Bruce, Janet, xiv
Brown, Robert, with Boston Reso-
lutes (1887), 135
Brown, William (executive, Chi-
cago Leland Giants) (1906), *98*
Buckner, Harry, 65, 129, 118; with
Brooklyn Royal Giants (1907),
88, 121–23, 125; with Chicago
Columbia Giants (1900), 28;
with Chicago Unions (1899), 26;
with Cuban X-Giants (1904–6),
33, 44, 60; with Philadelphia
Giants (1903–7), 40, 127–28,
146
Buffalo NY, xxviii, 76
Burlington PA, 132
Burns, Peter: with Chicago Co-
lumbia Giants (1899), 28; with
Page Fence Giants (1895), 24
Bustamante, Luis: with Brooklyn
Royal Giants (1907), 122, 125;
with Cuban Stars (1906–7), 91–
92, *93*, 124

Calvert TX, xl
Calvin, Floyd J. (journalist, *Pitts-
burgh Courier*), lxii, 143
Camden NJ, 58
Camps, Manuel (owner, Cuban
Stars, Santiago, Cuba) (1906),
91, 92
Carter, Charles ("Kid"), 65; with
Philadelphia Giants (1902–5),
31, 40, 44, *64*

Carvallo, ?, with Cuban Stars (1907), 124

"Casey At the Bat," 102, 105, 107

Castone, William, with Lincoln NE Giants (1890), 18

Catholic Protectory Grounds. *See* Protectory Oval, New York

Catto, Harry, with Cuban Giants (1889), 137

Chadwick, Bruce, xiv

Chalk, Ocania, xiv

Charleston, Oscar, xv

Charlottesville VA, 131

Chicago, American League, xxxvii, 118

Chicago American Giants (1910s–1920s), xxxii, xxxvii, xlii, liv, 143, 145, 152

Chicago Broad Ax, xlvi, 31

Chicago Columbia Giants, xxxix, 40, 63, 78, 152; of 1899, xxxv, 28, 38, 89; of 1900, xxxvi–xxxviii, 5, 38, 89, 146

Chicago Cricket Club, xxxvii

Chicago IL, xxxi, xxxvi, xxxvii, xli, 26, 28, 37, 38, 89, 146

Chicago Leland Giants, 26, 31, 33, 65, 118, 152; of 1905, 46; of 1907, xli, *xlv*, 119

Chicago, National League, xxxvi, 118, 142

Chicago Unions, 18, 26, 40, 63, 74; of 1884, 24, 26; of 1891, 26; of 1896, 26; of 1898, 89; of 1899, 28, 37–38, 89; of 1900, xxxvii, 38; of 1906, 31, 33; of 1907, 119

Chicago Union Giants (1905), 46

Cincinnati, National League, xxxiii, 14, 76, 135

Cincinnati OH, xxii, 14, 28, 119, 135

Clark, Dick, xi, xiv, 159

Clayton House Hotel, Wilmington DE, liii

Cleveland OH, 119

Cleveland Browns (1924), xliv, 148

Cleveland Gazette, xxii, xxvi, xxviii, xxix, xxx, 141–42

Cobb, Ty, xv, xlii

Coleman, A. A. (owner, Philadelphia Quaker Giants) (1908), *114*, 120

Collins, Nat, with New York Gorhams (1888), 14

Colored League. *See* League of Colored Base Ball Players

Colored Monarchs of York. *See* Monarchs of York

Columbia Park, Philadelphia (1906), xli

Columbia Social Club (owners, Chicago Columbia Giants) (1899–1900), xxxvii, 28, 152

Columbia Giants. *See* Chicago Columbia Giants

Columbus OH, xliv, 80, 147

Columbus OH Buckeyes (1920–24), 147

Comiskey, Charles, xxxvii, xlii

Comiskey Park, Chicago, xxxvii

Connecticut State League (1891), xxviii, xxx

Connor, John W. (owner, Brooklyn Giants), xxxix, xlvii–xlviii, 143; in 1906, xli, 31, *82*, 147; White's assessment of, 151

Cook, Walter (owner, Cuban Giants) (1886–87), 10, 14, 136, 149–50, 155

Cooperstown NY, xi, xvi, lxii, 154–55

Crane, Ed, injures Frank Grant (1887), 136

Crawford Grill, Pittsburgh (1930s), xxxix

Cuba, lx

Cuban Giants, xxii, xxiv, xxvi, xxxviii, 5, 111, 143, 155; of 1885, lviii, 8, 10, 134; of 1886, 10, 12, 130–33, 134, 149; of 1887, *xxiii*,

Cuban Giants (*cont.*)
lii, 14, 35, 36, 51, 76, 134–35,
149–50; of 1888, *xxv*, lvii–lviii,
14, 16, 36, 143; of 1889, 16, 36,
136, 164; of 1890 (Monarchs of
York), xxvi, xxvii, xxxv, 16, 18,
20, 144; of 1891 (Big Gorhams),
xxviii, xxx, 144–45, 166; of
1892, 20, 24; of 1893, 24, 145;
of 1894, 24, 37, 89, 145; of
1895, 24; of 1896 (Cuban
X-Giants), xxxv–xxxvi, 146; of
1896–1906 (*see* Genuine Cuban
Giants); origin of name, lviii–
lxi; rivalry with Cuban
X-Giants, xxxvi; use of "gibberish," lviii–lxi
Cuban Stars, Santiago, Cuba
(1905–6), 31, 33, 91
Cuban Stars, Havana, Cuba
(1906–7), 31, 33, 120
Cuban Stars, New York (1920s),
152
Cuban X-Giants, xlvii, 5, 65; of
1896, xxxv–xxxvi, 28, 37; of
1897, 37, 146; of 1898, 146; of
1899, 37–38, 146; of 1900,
xxxvii, 38; of 1901, xxxviii, 89,
146; of 1902, 89, 146; of 1903,
40, 42, 89, 146; of 1904, xl, xli,
42, 44, 46, 57, 60–62, 89; of
1905, *36*; of 1906, 31, 33, 46;
rivalry with Cuban Giants, 35–
36
Cushman, Charlie, rumored interest in signing black player
(1891), 139

Dabney, John and Lillian, xi, 169
Dabney, Milton, with Argyle Hotel
team (1885), 8, 169
Daniels, Harry (executive, Philadelphia Quaker Giants) (1908),
120
Davids, L. Robert ("Bob"), xi,
161–68

Davidson, Craig, xi
Davis, Ambrose (owner, New York
Gorhams) (1887–91), xxvi, xxx,
16, 20, 143, 145, 150
Davis, John, with Chicago Leland
Giants (1905–6), 65, 118
Day, Guy, with Argyle Hotel team
(1885), 8
Dayton OH, 152
Defiance team, Philadelphia
(1907), 119–20
Denver CO, xxxv
Detroit, National League, 14, 51,
136
Detroit MI, xxxi, xxxiii, xxxiv, xli,
152
Devoe, ?, with Philadelphia Giants
(1905), 55
Dixon, Phil, xiv
Dixon, Thomas Ryan (*The Clans-
man, The Leopard's Spots*), li,
liv
Douglas Club, Washington DC
(1880s), 130
Douglass Hall, Baltimore (1886–
87), xxii
DuBois, W.E.B. (*The Souls of
Black Folk*), lv
Duncan, Frank ("Pete"), with
Philadelphia Giants (1908), 147
Dunlap, Fred, 14, 132

Earl (Earle), Frank, with Genuine
Cuban Giants (1906), 33, 118,
129
Eastern Colored League (1920s),
xliv, 152–53
Eastern Interstate League (1890),
xxvii, xxviii, 165–66
Eastern League (1880s), 10, 54,
76, 134
Easton PA, xxvi, 36
Eggleston, William, with Argyle
Hotel team (1885), 8
Elizabeth NJ, 33
Elizabethport NJ, 123

Esquire, lix, lxi

Evans, John, with New York Gorhams (1888), 16

Evans, William, with Philadelphia Giants (1903), 40, 128

Excelsiors team, Philadelphia (1880s), xxxvii

Figarola, Jose, with Cuban Stars (1907), 124

Fig'ralla. *See* Figarola, Jose

Findlay oh, *xxxiii*

Findlay Daily Courier, xxxi

Findlay Colored Western Giants (1895), xxxii

Fisher, ?, with Philadelphia Giants (1908), 147

Footes, Robert, 118; with Brooklyn Royal Giants (1906), *90;* with Chicago Unions (1899), 37; with Philadelphia Giants (1903–4), 40, 44, 60

Fort Plain ny, xvi

Fort Wayne in, xxxi, 5

Foster, Andrew ("Rube"), 65, 118; and Chicago American Giants, xxxii, xxxvii, 143, 145; and John McGraw, lvi; founds Negro National League (1920), xxiv, xliv, xlviii, 147, 152; "How to Pitch," xlii, 96, 99–100; with Chicago Leland Giants (1907), xli, *xlv;* with Cuban X-Giants (1903), xl, 40, 42, 44, 46, 146; with Philadelphia Giants (1904–6), 55, 57, 58, 60, 61, 62, *66,* 89, 146–47

Fowler (born Jackson), John W. ("Bud"), xvii, 10, 74, 110, 137–38, 150, 154–55; and League of Colored Base Ball Players (1887), xxii; first black professional player (1878), xvi, 74; minor league statistics, 161; organizes Page Fence Giants (1895), xxxi, xxxiv, 24; use of

shin guards, 137; victim of baseball violence, 137; with Binghamton ny (1887), xix; with Findlay oh (1894), *xxxiii;* with Keokuk ia (1885), *xvii;* with Lynn ma (1878), xvi

Francis, Bill, 118; with Breakers Hotel team (1914), *xlv;* with Philadelphia Giants (1906–7), xli, 33, 121, 123, 128

Freihoffer, William (president, International League of Colored Baseball Teams) (1906), 33, *106*

Frye (Fry), John ("Jack"), xvii; minor league statistics, 161; with Cuban Giants (1886–89), *xxiii, xxv,* 10, 12, *25,* 135, 136; with Monarchs of York (1890), *xxvii*

G. A. Rabbit. *See* Ball, George Walter

Garcia, Antonio, Cuban player, 92; with Genuine Cuban Giants, *32*

Garvey, Marcus, xlix

Gatewood, Bill, 65; with Chicago Leland Giants (1906), 33; with Cuban X-Giants (1906), 33

Gehrig, Lou, xv

Genuine Cuban Giants ("Original/Famous Cuban Giants"), 65, 74; of 1896, 37; of 1899, 28; of 1900, xxxvii–xxxviii, 28; of 1906, 31, 33; of 1908, 120; rivalry with Cuban Giants, xxxvi

Georgia Rabbit. *See* Ball, George Walter

Glens Falls ny, 20

Globes team, Bellaire oh (1880s), xxi–xxii

Gordon, Bruce, rumored interest of Milwaukee in signing (1891), 139

Gordon, Sam, with Genuine Cuban Giants (1905–6), as "comedian," 74

Hilldale Club, Philadelphia, 143, 152

Hoboken NJ, 125, 144

Hoch, L. W. (co-owner, Page Fence Giants) (1895), xxxii, 24, 152–53

Hogan, Lawrence D., xi, 169

Holland, William ("Billy"), 26, 65, 118; with Brooklyn Royal Giants (1906), *87*, 121, 123; with Chicago Unions (1899), 37; with Page Fence Giants (1895), 24

Holmes, Benjamin Franklin ("Ben"), 111; early career, 130; with Cuban Giants (1885–88), *xxiii, xxv*, 8, 10, *11*, 12, 132, 135; with Philadelphia Orions (1885), lxi

Holway, John B., xiv

Hopkins, George, with Chicago Unions (1899), 26, 37, 63

Horn, William: with Algona Brownies (1903), 40; with Chicago Unions (1899), 26, 37; with Philadelphia Giants (1904), 44, 62

Hot Springs AR, 78

Hotel Champlain, Bluff Point NY, xxxi, 145

Howard, Charles, with Cuban X-Giants (1899), 37

Hughbanks ("Ubanks"), Hugh, with Lincoln NE Giants (1890), 18

Human,? (owner, Keystone Giants, Philadelphia) (1907), 119

Hyde, Harry, with Chicago Unions (1899), 26, 37, 47

Independent League (1903–4), 146, 147

Indianapolis IN, xxxii, 14, 119, 152

Indianapolis A.B.C.s (1910s–1920s), 143

International Association (1888), xix

International League of Colored Base Ball Teams (1906), 31, 33, 120

International League (1880s), xli, 110, 137–38, 140, 147, 149; 1887 season, xviii–xxi, 65, 76, 139

Jackson, Andrew ("Andy"), xxiv; with Big Gorhams (1891), xxx, 20, 89; with Cuban X-Giants (1899), 37; with Monarchs of York (1890), 18; with New York Gorhams (1888), 16

Jackson, John W. *See* Fowler, John W.

Jackson, Oscar, xxiv; with Big Gorhams, xxx, 20, 89; with Monarchs of York (1890), 18; with New York Gorhams (1887–88), 16, 36

Jackson, Randolph, with Oswego NY (1887), xix

Jackson, Robert ("Bob"), xxiv; with Chicago Unions (1899), 37, *50*; with New York Gorhams (1887–88), 16, 35

Jackson, William: with Cuban X-Giants (1903), 40, 44, 60, 62; with Monarchs of York (1890), *xxvii*

Jacksonville FL, lxi, 65

James, Willie ("Nux"), with Philadelphia Giants (1907), 121, 123, 125, 127, 147

Jersey City NJ, xxviii, 134, 141–42

Johnson, Dick. *See* Johnson, Richard

Johnson, Byron Bancroft ("Ban"), xxii, 144

Johnson, George, Jr. ("Chappie/Chappy"), 118; with Brooklyn Royal Giants (1906), 33, *86*, 121, 123; with Chicago Columbia Giants (1899–1900), 28, *95*; with Chicago Union Giants (1905),

Miller, Joe: with Chicago Columbia Giants (1899), 28; with Lincoln NE Giants (1890), 18; with Page Fence Giants (1895), xxxv, 24

Millville NJ team (1880s), 131

Milliner, Eugene, with Brooklyn Royal Giants (1907), 121–23

Milwaukee, American Association, 139

Molina, Augustin ("Tinti"), 92

Monarch Bicycle Company, xxxii–xxxiii

Monarchs of York PA (1890), xxvi–xxvii, *xxvii*, 5, 18, 20, 144, 165

Mongin, Sam, with Philadelphia Giants (1907), 122, 124–26

Monitors team, Brooklyn NY (1880s), xxxvii

Monroe, William S. ("Bill"), 118; as "comedian," 74, *85*; with Brooklyn Royal Giants, 33, 122, 125; with Chicago Unions (1899), 26, 37; with Philadelphia Giants (1903–6), xxxvii, xl, 40, 44, 55, 58, 60, 62, 89; with Philadelphia Quaker Giants (1906), 147

Moore, Harry W. ("Mike"), 26, 118; with Algona Brownies (1903), 40; with Chicago Unions (1899), 37; with Cuban X-Giants (1904), 44, 60, 62; with Philadelphia Giants (1905), 55, 58, 89

Mortin, R., with Argyle Hotel team (1885), 8

Munoz, Joseito ("Joe"), with Cuban Stars, Havana (1907), 124

Munroe, William S. *See* Monroe, William S.

Mutrie, Jim, attempts to sign Stovey, Walker (1887), lvii

Mutuals team, Washington DC (1880s), xxxvii

Myers, "Lefty" (manager, Defiance team, Philadelphia) (1907), 120

National Agreement, xxii

National Association of Colored Base Ball Clubs of the United States and Cuba (1906), xlviii, 91

National Association for the Advancement of Colored People, 1

National Baseball Hall of Fame Museum and Library, xi, xiv, lxii

National Colored League. *See* League of Colored Base Ball Players

National League, xvii, xix, xxii, xxxiii, xxxiv, 12, 49, 76, 78, 110, 111, 120, 128

National League of Colored Base Ball Clubs (1908), 119

Neale, Dick. *See* Johnson, Richard

Nebraska State League (1890), 18

Negro a Beast, The (Charles Carroll), li

Negro League Players Association, xiv

Negro Leagues Baseball Museum, xi

Negro National League (1920s), xlii, xliv, 152

Nelson, John, xxiv, 118; with Genuine Cuban X-Giants (1899), 37; with New York Gorhams (1887–89), 14, 31, 35, 36; with Philadelphia Giants (1902–3), 31, 40, *42*

New Brunswick NS, Canada, 20

New Castle PA, 74

New England League (1905), 147

New York, American Association, 131, 134

New York, American League, xxxix, xli, 147

New York, National League,

xxxviii, lvi, lvii, lxi, 49, 51, 76,
78, 118, 131, 141–42
New York Age, xlvi, lx, 134–35,
136
(New York) *Amsterdam News,* xlvi,
149–53
New York Black Yankees (1940s),
xlvii
New York Boston Giants (1912),
147
New York Giants, black team
(1906, 1908), 31, 120
New York Gorhams, xxxvi, 143–
44; of 1887, xxiii, 12, 14; of
1888, xxiv, 16, 36, 150; of 1889,
xxvi, 5, 18, 36–37, 165; of 1891
(*see* Big Gorhams [1891])
New York Lincoln Giants, 143; in
Eastern Colored League
(1920s), 152–53; of 1911, xlii,
147
New York NY, xlvi, 12, 147
New York Quaker Giants (1906),
31
(New York) *Sun,* lviii
(Newark) *Daily Journal,* lvii
Newark Bears, white team (1904–
5), xli, 147
Newark NJ, xix–xx, 54, 134, 141,
147
Newark Stars, Eastern Colored
League (1926), xliv, 148
Newburgh NY, 16, 35, 150
Nichols, Charles, with Argyle
Hotel team (1885), 8
Norfolk VA, xxiv, 144
Norristown PA, 16
Northwestern League (1884), xvi
Noyle, Dick. *See* Johnson, Richard

Oberlin College, xlix
Ohio State League (1887), xviii,
xxi, xxiv, 5, 76, 79, 144
Ormond Hotel team, Palm Beach
FL, 128–29
O'Neil, John ("Buck"), xiv

Original Cuban Giants. *See* Genuine Cuban Giants
Orions, Philadelphia. *See* Philadelphia Orions
O'Rourke, John A. (secretary, International League of Colored
Base Ball Teams) (1906), 33
Our Home Colony. See Walker,
Moses Fleetwood

Page Fence Giants, Adrian MI,
xxxvii, xxxix, xlvii, liv, 5, 31; of
1895, xxxi–xxxv, 24, 146, 152;
of 1896, 37; of 1898, xxxv; become Chicago Columbia Giants
(1899), 28, 38
Page Woven Wire Fence Company, xxxii
Palimino, Emilio, 92
Palm Beach FL, 128–29
Palmyra MI, xxxv
Parago, George. *See* Parego,
George
Parego, George: early career, 131;
with Cuban Giants (1885–88),
xxiii, xxv, lxi, 8, 14, *19,* 35, 131,
132, 135; with Keystone Athletics (1885), lxi, 131
Parsons, Augustus S. ("Gus," manager, Page Fence Giants) (1895–
98), xxxiii, 24, 152
Patterson, John W. ("Pat"), 118;
with Brooklyn Royal Giants
(1906), 33, 122–23, 125; with
Chicago Columbia Giants
(1899–1900), xxxvii, 28, 97,
146; with Cuban X-Giants
(1904), 44, 46, 60, 62; with
Lincoln NE Giants (1890), 18;
with Page Fence Giants (1895),
24; with Philadelphia Giants
(1903), 40, 146
Payne, Andrew ("Jap"): with
Cuban X-Giants (1903), 40;
with Philadelphia Giants (1902,
1904), xl, 31, 44, 60, 62

Peary ("Commodore Perry"), Admiral Robert E., 154
Pell, Frank, with New York Gorhams (1888), 16
Penn Park Athletic Club, white team, York PA (1903), 54
"Pennsylvania League" (1889-90), xxvi, xxvii, 5, 16, 18, 36
Pennsylvania State League (1887), 134
Perez, ?, 96
Pershing, General John, xlvii
Perry, Commodore. See Peary, Admiral Robert E.
Peters, W. S. (co-owner, Chicago Unions) (1890s-1900s), 26, 45, 152; White's assessment of, 152
Peterson, Robert W. (*Only the Ball Was White*), xi, xiv, xx-xxi
Petway, Bruce, 118; with Breakers Hotel team, Palm Beach FL (1914), *xlv;* with Chicago Leland Giants (1906-10), xlii; with Cuban X-Giants (1906), 33; with Philadelphia Giants (1907), xli, 121-26, 147; with Royal Palm Hotel team, Palm Beach FL (1907), 129
Philadelphia, American Association, lvii, 131, 134
Philadelphia, American League, xxxviii, xli, 33, 49, 51, 118, 126-28
Philadelphia Giants, xlviii, 5, 65, 118, 143; of 1902, xxxviii, xl, 31, 77, 146; of 1903, xl, 40, 42, 51, 146; of 1904, xl-xli, 42, 44, 46, 58, 60-62, 146-47; of 1905, xxxi, xli, 54-55, *60*, 85, 89, 147; of 1906, xli, 33, 46, 49, 51, 58, *111*, 147; of 1907, xli, 119, 120-28, 147; of 1908, xli-xlii, 147
Philadelphia *Inquirer*, 157
Philadelphia *Item*, xlviii, 31, 49, 53, 146

Philadelphia Orions team (1885), lx, 8, 134
Philadelphia PA, xxiv, xxxix, xlvii, lxiii, 8, 12, 131, 134, 149, 152
Philadelphia Professionals (1906), 33
Philadelphia Pythians team (1880s), xxxvii, 144
Philadelphia Quaker Giants (1906-9), xli, 33, 120, 147
Philadelphia *Record*, 136
Philadelphia *Tribune*, xlviii, 31, 69
Pittsburgh, National League, 14
(Pittsburgh) *Courier*, xxi, xlvi, xlviii, li, lxi, lxii, 143-48
Pittsburgh Crawfords (1930s), xxxix
Pittsburgh Keystones: of 1887, xviii, xxi, xxii-xxiv, 5, 12, 14, 143-44, 150; of 1888, xxiv, 16, 36, 150; of 1892, xxxi
Pittsburgh PA, xxii-xxiii, 12, 119, 144
Plattsburg NY, 110
Poles, Spotswood: with Breakers Hotel team (1914), *xlv;* with Philadelphia Giants (1908), xlii
Post Office Club, Washington DC, 132
Powers, Pat, steals Stovey from Cuban Giants (1886), 141-42
Prats (Pratz), E., with Cuban Stars (1907), 92, 124
Princeton NJ, xxviii
Providence RI, 131
Protectory Oval (home grounds, New York Lincoln Giants), 153

Quaker Giants, New York. See New York Quaker Giants
Quaker Giants, Philadelphia. See Philadelphia Quakers

Rabbit, Georgia. See Ball, George Walter
Ramos, ?, with Cuban Stars (1907), 124

Trusty, Shepard ("Shep"): with Cuban Giants (1886–88), *xxiii, xxv,* lx, 8, 10, 131; with Philadelphia Orions (1885), 131
Tygiel, Jules, xiv

Ubanks. *See* Hughbanks, Hugh
Union Giants. *See* Chicago Union Giants
Uniques team, Brooklyn NY (1880s), xxxvii
United States Supreme Court, lii–liii
University of Michigan, xlix
University of Vermont, 20

Vactor, John: with Cuban Giants (1886), 132; with New York Gorhams (1887–88), xxiv, 16
Valdez, Rogelio, 92
Van Dyke, Fred, with Page Fence Giants (1895), 24
Vardaman, James K., 1, 76
Vermont, lvi
Virgin Islands, lx

Waddell, Rube, xxxv, 65, 118
Wagner, Honus, xxxv, xxxix, 118
Walker, George (entertainer), xlvii
Walker, Moses Fleetwood ("Fleet"), xxi, lxii, 10, 110, 137, 149; first black major league player, Toledo OH (1884), xvi–xvii, 76; minor league statistics, 161; *Our Home Colony* (1908), xlix–l; with Newark NJ (1887), xix–xxi, lvii, 76; with Syracuse NY (1888), *xix;* with Toledo OH (1883–84), xvi–xvii, *xviii,* 76
Walker, Weldy Wilberforce, xviii, 76; protests color line, xxi, 79–81; with Akron OH (1887), 76, 79, *104;* with Pittsburgh Keystones (1887), 14; with Toledo OH (1884), xvii
Ward, John Montgomery, attempts

to sign Stovey, Walker (1887), lvii, 76
Washington, Tom, with Philadelphia Giants (1905–6), 58, 65, 89
Washington DC, 12, 130, 131, 144, 149
Washington DC Potomacs team (1920s), 152
(Waterbury CT) *American,* xxviii, xxx
Watkins, John ("Pop"): as "comedian," 74; with Genuine Cuban Giants (1906–7), *30,* 74, 120; with Pop Watkins Stars, New York (1908), 120
Watson, Tom, l
Weehauken NJ, 37
Western Interstate League (1895), xxxi, 5, 146
Western League (1890), 18
Wheeling WV, xxi, xxiv, lii, 5, 14, 144
Wheeling WV Keystones (1887), 144
"When Casey Slugged the Ball," 107–8, 110
White, Solomon ("King Solomon," "Sol"), 144, 154–55; ability as player, xxiv–xxvi; on ability of Big Gorhams, xxviii, 20, 85, 89; on baseball "comedians," 71, 74; on black players with major league ability, 110–11, 118; on black press, 153, 155; on Bright, J. M., xxxvi, 150–51; career summary, 143–48, 159; on color line, lii, lv–lvii, 74–81, 111, 118; on commercialization of black baseball, 153; on Connor, John W., 151; on Cuban players, 89–96; education of, xlvi–xlvii, 5; on fans, 71, 74; on Foster, Rube, 55, 57, 152; on Govern, S. K., 150; on Grant, Frank, 103, 110–11; on greatest

Wilmington DE Giants (1906), 31, 33, 46
Wilson, Ed: with Cuban X-Giants (1899, 1903), 37, 40; with Philadelphia Giants (1907), 122, 125, 127–28
Wilson, George, 63, 65, 118; "bronzed Wadell," 65; with Chicago Columbia Giants (1899), 28; with Chicago Union Giants (1905), 46; with Page Fence Giants (1895), xxxv
Wilson, Ray: with Cuban X-Giants (1903), 40, 41; with Philadelphia Giants (1907), 121–28
Wilson, Woodrow, li
Woodward, C. Vann (*The Strange Career of Jim Crow*), lii

Wright, George, 118; with Brooklyn Royal Giants (1906), 33; with Philadelphia Quaker Giants (1906), 33
Wyatt, David, with Chicago Unions (1890s), 26, *48*

Xenia OH, xlvi

Yankee Stadium, xlvi
York PA, xxvi, xxxv, 16, 18, 54
York Gazette, xxvi
York Monarchs. *See* Monarchs of York
Young, Lt. Col. Charles, xlvii

Zanesville OH, 80

Library of Congress Cataloging-in-Publication Data
White, Sol, b. 1868.
    [History of colored base ball, with other documents on the early
Black game, 1886–1936]
    Sol White's history of colored base ball, with other documents on the
early Black game, 1886–1936 / compiled and introduced by Jerry
Malloy.
        p.   cm.
    Rev. ed. of: Sol. White's official base ball guide. 1907.
    Includes bibliographical references.
    ISBN 0-8032-4771-0 (alk. paper)
    1. Negro leagues—United States—History.   2. Baseball—United
States—History.   I. Malloy, Jerry, 1946–   .   II. White, Sol, b. 1868.
Official base ball guide.   III. Title.   IV. Title: Sol White's history of
colored baseball.
GV863.A1W448   1995
796.357′0973—dc20
                                                                    94-20992
                                                                        CIP